WITHOUT APOLOGY

WITHOUT APOLOGY

Reflections on Independent Education

FREDERICK C. CALDER

NYSAIS

Published by the New York State Association of Independent Schools

NYSAIS
12 Jay Street
Schenectady, New York 12305
518-346-5662
www.nysais.org

ISBN-13: 978-0-615-13376-8

Editor: Lucy Schneider
Managing Editor: Laura L. Morris
Designer: Liz Driesbach
Printer: The Maple-Vail Book Manufacturing Group

Printed in the U.S.A.

WITHOUT APOLOGY

Frederick C. Calder

PREFACE

It is safe to say that being a teacher and an administrator in an independent school has permanently shaped my habits. Although I am now retired from full-time work, it is still impossible to read a book or an article, to see a museum exhibition or a film, or to hear about a workshop without thinking of colleagues or students. Thus when I heard Fred Calder was planning to retire as executive director of the New York State Association of Independent Schools, I immediately saw the need to compile two decades of his bulletins addressed to the heads of member schools in a format that would allow his wisdom to be available to a wider audience—new heads of schools, trustees, faculty, parents—virtually anyone interested in independent education.

Originally published in the *Bulletin of the New York State Association of Independent Schools*, Fred's writings are cannily refreshing and insightful. Reading and rereading these texts with a selective eye revealed to me Fred's consistency of thought over time, yet also his capacity for thinking anew. The decision to organize his essays thematically rather than chronologically is intended to make Fred's voice readily accessible to anyone seeking perspective on subjects ranging from the essential nature of independent schools to the challenges confronting their leaders. Organizing the bulletins by theme proved surprisingly daunting, as several essays seemed to defy categorization. My decisions on such questions were ultimately supported by Andrew McLaren, associate executive editor of NYSAIS, whose sense of humor, intelligence, and steady presence enabled me to navigate the book's development with a sense of calm assurance. I am also grateful to my editor,

Laura Morris, whose clear thinking and faithful attention to organization and detail enabled this project to remain true to its intention. Lois Bailey and Annie Nark, in the NYSAIS office, must be thanked as well for their immediate response to my every request.

This book could not have been realized without the support of the trustees of NYSAIS, who have undertaken this publication in honor of Fred's retirement. I am grateful for their trust and also for the contributions of the former presidents of NYSAIS whose introductions to each section of the book offer an engaging variety of voices.

Most of all, I wish to express my gratitude to Fred Calder for allowing me to pursue this project. It has been a privilege to be immersed in his writings. Each of us who has worked with Fred knows the power of his insight, wisdom, equanimity, and integrity. And each of us knows the power of his abiding faith in our work. It is my hope that this volume contributes in some small way to extending the Calder legacy, while Fred himself enjoys his retirement years. *Salud*!

LUCY SCHNEIDER
Rudolf Steiner School

INTRODUCTION

Without Apology is a compilation of some of the pieces Frederick Calder has written for the *Bulletin of the New York State Association of Independent Schools* over the past twenty years. Each section of the book is introduced by one of the NYSAIS Board of Trustees presidents with whom Fred has worked. The first section is on independence: what it means, why it is valuable, and how it has played out in our schools. This is followed by a section that broadens the perspective, looking at the politics of education, both in national and state contexts. In the third part Fred examines the cultures and communities of our schools, which are sometimes idiosyncratic, sometimes inspiring, and always interesting. And the final section develops his philosophy and theory of leadership. The individual essays are trenchant, witty, delightful, and wise. Collectively, they exemplify Fred's own take on the essence of good leadership, which is to interpret reality in ways that will make people listen, understand, and then act.

Frederick Calder was born at home—which was 35 Prospect Park West in Brooklyn—on July 19, 1935. He reports that the doctor submitted a huge bill, which his father promptly contested, giving him an early push toward the fiscal prudence he would later urge on others. His grandfather was Congressman and Senator from New York for over twenty years, so he had politics in his blood. Nurture followed nature. As the second of four children, he learned early both how to stand up for himself and how to duck and weave.

After a few years the family moved to Garden City, New York, and then to Concord, Massachusetts, for no apparent reason other than his mother's strong belief that Long Island was unsafe in the upcoming atomic age. Fred attended Middlesex School in Concord as a day student, and then Harvard University, where he majored in Byzantine and Russian history. He has since made it to Constantinople, but not yet to Russia.

After Harvard Fred spent seven years teaching at Belmont Hill in Belmont, Massachusetts, and then became head of the Town School in New York City at the tender age of thirty. He spent five entirely successful years at Town, followed by sixteen more as head of Germantown Friends School in Philadelphia. Then, in 1986, he took on his present post as executive director of NYSAIS. Fred has three sons, Grant, Wynn, and Peter, all of whom are in one way or another involved with education, and five grandchildren.

I was on the search committee that brought Fred to NYSAIS and have been a close friend ever since. For the last three years I have also been his associate executive director—which might well have been a recipe for the end of our friendship, but the opposite has been the case. We see eye to eye on most things and laugh about the rest. It is worth noting that two out of the three other NYSAIS staff members have been with Fred throughout his tenure. Barbara Swanson and Lois Bailey are in charge of professional-development activities and the NYSAIS accreditation process, respectively. They share a profound gratitude that they have been lucky enough to spend twenty years working with Fred, a feeling that is only accentuated by his being equally (and equally deservedly) grateful in reverse.

Leaders in independent schools have benefited greatly from the forceful statements Fred has made not only in the *Bulletin* but also on our behalf in Albany. In personal terms, however, they would agree he is defined much more by his ability to listen to and laugh with others than by any desire to tell them what to think. Indeed, the essence of his relationship with his many friends and colleagues is the sense on all of our parts that he hears us with care and clarity. The result is that we feel *known* by him. It is hard to imagine a greater gift.

As NYSAIS executive director, Fred is by definition responsible for the opinions here expressed—but not for the selection of what to include and what to omit. That task has been brilliantly accomplished by Lucy Schneider, former faculty chair of the Rudolf Steiner School in New York City, supported in every way by the NYSAIS Board of Trustees. She has managed this book through to completion, taking charge of every aspect of its publication. Without Fred it could, of course, not exist; nor could it without Lucy.

Fred does indeed speak without apology. He is the master of the declarative sentence, believing that reality is best interpreted and understood through a clear point of view. This, as he would be the first to point out, is no guarantee of wisdom. The world, after all, would be a great deal better off, if the points of view of some of our past and present leaders had a little more uncertainty mixed in. What distinguishes Fred is that he does not allow today's declarative sentence to become tomorrow's prior conclusion. Not only does he have an unusual ability to arrive at conclusions, rather than start from them, he demonstrates, in piece after piece, that matters of seriousness are best dealt with by those who don't take themselves too seriously. So listen to the voice of Fred Calder, and enjoy!

ANDREW MCLAREN
Associate Executive Director and
former Board President, NYSAIS

INDEPENDENT SCHOOLS

INTRODUCTION

Rightfully, this volume opens with a section celebrating the virtues of independence. In the selected bulletin essays, Fred examines the bedrock and defining character of our association's schools. They are first and foremost *independent* schools, and, in the Fred Calder philosophy, independence is the essential quality for excellence in education.

The governance and operation of our schools harmonize with the great historical American value of local control, the autonomy enjoyed by our institutions to determine their individual destinies. In a penetrating review of the legal foundation of independent education, Fred analyzes the federal cases (*Dartmouth College v. Woodward* and *Pierce v. the Society of Sisters*) and the state case (*Packer Collegiate Institute v. University of the State of New York*) that secured the legal basis of our independence. Collectively, this jurisprudence is our shield against what Fred ominously terms the "monolith" of a deadening public educational system that is restrictive, bureaucratic, and standardized. Independent education has defended its very existence in the courts, prevailing in that effort.

But a secure right to independence does not fully define its deepest nature. For Fred, obligation accompanies independence. Independent schools present choice to families in the educational marketplace, and they do so because they pursue unique and diverse missions, serve particular student bodies, and are financed by and accountable to their distinct constituencies. Independence grants latitude: to differentiate, to make distinctions, to locally define a superior educational program. To forego these opportunities would be to forsake the full potential of independence.

The final two bulletins in this section address the paradox of schools that cherish their individual freedom yet also join an organization committed to group action. For Fred, the benefits of independence flourish in an association of schools that, however distinct individually, are like-minded in their belief in the sanctity of the ideal of independence. A valid and credible process of accreditation by peers, as well as a reputation for fair-mindedness and for upholding principles of good practice, strengthen each member school in the eyes of the public.

The Calder legacy includes both the legal vigilance necessary to preserve independence and the strong association that guides its fruits in practice. Through the words of these bulletins, Fred bequeaths an enduring philosophy of independence to future generations of school leaders.

CHARLES F. HERTRICK
Head, Allendale Columbia School

THE POINT
OF INDEPENDENCE

Bulletin 222, October 1997

Independent schooling doesn't seem to matter in most of the world. In Europe or its former colonies where government, often heavily, subsidizes private schools, they toe the line. National curricula and national examinations prevail. The old adage "Follow the money" holds sway. If government is paying preponderantly for schooling, then government decides that which is taught. What surprises Americans is that no one seems to object very much in other developed countries to centralized control. Presumably, what baffles Europeans and others about Americans is that we care so passionately about local control.

Compared to the rest of the planet, public education in America still enjoys a fair degree of local autonomy. But much of it has become illusory. State mandates and money, union contracts, and tenure laws have sharply reduced authority. Ask the members of any board of education and they will tell you that on the big issues their hands are largely tied. The current furor about low standards and widespread mediocrity in the public schools begs an answer. Some people think that the decline of the public schools is in direct proportion to the decline of local control in fact, not just theory. The argument goes that if you're not accountable directly to your immediate patrons, quality eventually drops. Seems obvious, doesn't it? Or does it?

As the centralizing forces in Washington and state capitals do their will, the last bastions of local autonomy, private schools, rebel. To be independent means taking responsibility for your successes and for your messes. It means taking risks and accepting the consequences. Clearly, the more centralized the system, the easier it is to duck. Contracts and laws limit changes in personnel. Mandated courses and curricula leave little room for new programs. Required subject-area tests stifle classroom creativity. It's the bureaucrat's dream to be able to say, "I'm sorry, but there's nothing we can do about it." It's much harder, of course, to be independent, to be accountable every day, and, oddly, some think, we actually *like* being responsible for all of the education we offer. We believe we know more about our business than anyone else, and we demand the freedom of choice to deliver what it is we know. And in our Jeffersonian souls, we are certain of the virtues of local control and independence.

THE ROOTS
OF INDEPENDENCE

Bulletins 225–27, February–April 1998

Though seldom acknowledged, the independence of our schools rests on two seminal Supreme Court cases, without which we would be, effectively, creatures of the state. At a time when the gathering elements of conflict may once again be leading toward another great judicial clash, it is useful to recall what has gone before. Because it is upon these precedents and their meaning in our time that the next decision will be based.

The first great case was *Dartmouth College v. Woodward*, argued by Daniel Webster before John Marshall's Supreme Court in 1819. Dartmouth had existed as a private educational institution governed by a self-perpetuating board of trustees since 1769. In 1816 the New Hampshire legislature passed a law that recast Dartmouth's charter, removing its trustees and replacing them with overseers appointed by the governor. By this act the legislature had essentially turned Dartmouth into a public university under government control. The trustees sued.

The question before the Court was whether Dartmouth's charter was a contract protected by article 1, section 10 of the Constitution. In his famous peroration Daniel Webster spoke thus: "For the question is simply this: shall our State legislatures be allowed to take *that which is not their own*, to turn it from its original use, and apply it to such ends or purposes as they, in their discretion, shall see fit?

Sir, you may destroy this little institution....You may put it out; but if you do, you must carry through your work! You must extinguish, one after another, all these great lights of science, which, for more than a century, have thrown their radiance over our Land! It is, Sir, as I have said, a small college. And yet *there are those who love it....* Sir, I know not how others may feel, but, for myself, when I see my alma mater surrounded, like Caesar in the senate house, by those who are reiterating stab upon stab, I will not, for this right hand, have her say to me, and you also, my son!'"

Speaking for the Court, the chief justice wrote, "A corporation is an artificial being, invisible, intangible, and existing only in the contemplation of the law.... It possesses only those properties which the charter of its creation confers upon it.... Among the most important are immortality, and.... individuality. By these means, a perpetual succession of individuals are capable of acting for the promotion of a particular object, like one immortal being." Clearly, the implications of *Dartmouth* went far beyond the fate of private educational institutions, but, in this case, the point was made. The charter of a private school or college is a contract that cannot be abrogated by the state. So long as it fulfills the declared purposes of its charter and otherwise operates in a legal fashion, the state may not deprive it of its character or its property.

The message of *Dartmouth* goes beyond even this. It advocates that private schools are contractual, not constitutional, entities. They exist independently by contract with the state, and they perform, in turn, their educational function by contract with the families that employ their services. Through contract, private schools determine the conditions of attendance, the standards of behavior, and the academic program. They are not, unless they wish to be, democratic institutions. The Dartmouth College case provided the bedrock on which the independence and freedom of action of our schools rest.

More than a hundred years later, in June 1925, an equally important case was decided by the Supreme Court when the Society of Sisters of the Holy Names of Jesus and Mary and the Hill Military Academy brought suit against Walter Pierce, the governor of the state of Oregon. In the history of judicature this case has become known as *Pierce v. the Society of Sisters.*

In November 1922 the voters of Oregon adopted through initiative the Compulsory Education Act, which required every parent or guardian to send children between eight and sixteen years of age to a local public school. Failure to do so constituted a misdemeanor punishable by fines and/or imprisonment. Both the Society of Sisters and Hill Military Academy had long operated schools under the laws of Oregon. Two fundamental questions were at stake. First, do parents have the right to direct the education of their children by choosing who will teach them and where they will be taught? Second, can the state destroy the business and property of a private school by forcing its patrons to go elsewhere?

Justice McReynolds delivered the Court's opinion. After noting, "No question is raised concerning the power of the State reasonably to regulate all schools," McReynolds went on to say, "We think it entirely plain that the Act of 1922 unreasonably interferes with the liberty of parents and guardians to direct the upbringing and education of children under their control.... The fundamental theory of liberty upon which all governments in this Union repose excludes any general power of the State to standardize its children by forcing them to accept instruction from public teachers only. The child is not the mere creature of the State; those who nurture him and direct his destiny have the right, coupled with the high duty, to recognize and prepare him for additional obligations." The Court also held that enforcement of the Compulsory Education Act would do irreparable harm to the business and property of private schools. Thus it was declared null and void.

While *Dartmouth* established the right of private institutions to exist in perpetuity, *Pierce* asserted the right of parents to choose the educational setting for their children. State power was curbed by forbidding the erection of a monolithic educational system that all must attend. Upon these two critical decisions rests most of the constitutional protection private schools still enjoy.

But neither decision denied the state the right to regulate private schools. On the contrary, in *Pierce,* Justice McReynolds wrote:

"No question is raised concerning the power of the State reasonably to regulate all schools, to inspect, supervise and examine them, their teachers and pupils; to require . . . that certain studies plainly essential to good citizenship must be taught, and that nothing be taught which is manifestly inimical to the public welfare." Since 1925 the state and private schools have struggled to determine the line between reasonable and unreasonable regulation.

In 1945 the State of New York drew a line. An act of the legislature required that all nonsectarian private elementary schools apply for registration and be subject to regulation by the commissioner of education. Packer Collegiate Institute refused to apply and, joined by several sister schools, contested the law on constitutional grounds. Packer lost in the first instance and again lost unanimously at the appellate level. Finally, in 1948, Packer took the case to New York's highest tribunal, the Court of Appeals. On July 16, 1948, the Court struck down the Compulsory Registration Act by a 4–2 vote. But it was a close call. If one judge had voted the other way, the decision of the Appellate Division would have stood, and registration would have been the order of the day. Close though it may have been, much of our schools' freedom of action and independence has rested on the Packer case for the last half century.

Nevertheless, Packer was decided on narrow grounds. The Court did not say that the legislature could not regulate private schools. To the contrary, it noted that, "The Legislature, under the police power, has a limited right to regulate such schools in the public interest." What the Court actually decided was that the legislature could not delegate *broad, unspecified* regulatory power to the commissioner of education, and thus the act was unconstitutional. When New York, mindful of *Packer*, introduced high-school registration some years later, it was, theoretically, on a voluntary basis. But unless a school is registered, it cannot receive certain services and, most importantly, cannot confer legal diplomas. So much for volunteerism. The nose of the camel enters the tent in devious ways.

So the point of this legal exposition is to say that the freedom of choice and action we enjoy as schools occupies a shifting space between government's limited but substantial power to regulate all precollegiate education and our constitutional right to exist and function independently. As various political forces sweep through the nation, the state tries repeatedly in the name of reform to bring the private schools to heel. Our schools, of course, have three choices. They may simply accede. They may negotiate. Or they may practice civil disobedience. In the real world what we actually do is to operate somewhere between negotiation and disobedience. There is a venerable tradition in human affairs that the way to live with bureaucracy is to acknowledge it, on the one hand, and to ignore it, on the other. (Confucius must have said something like this.) But when intrusion becomes intolerable, and our schools are on the verge of losing their identity, we will once again take our case to the highest tribunal—or else hand over our individuality and our independence to the monolith.

THE RIGHT
TO BE DIFFERENT

Bulletin 111, September 1986

One of my first assignments for NYSAIS was to testify at the Annual Legislative Conference of the Board of Regents on September 5 in Albany. It was an opportunity once more to think through our mission as schools and to reassert, as we must continually do, what we believe and why we exist. Excerpts from my testimony follow.

Some may ask why this relatively small group of schools bands together in a statewide association, why we bother to appear here today, why we work so hard to stay healthy. And the answer is that regardless of philosophy or method, our schools have discovered again and again the best education of the young springs from a direct compact between family and teacher in which both are accountable and neither is unfairly restricted. What we cherish as independent schools is not our isolation from the public sector, but our right to decide with our constituencies how and when and where we shall deliver our cultural heritage. And that is what the effort is all about.

We understand too that we do not exist in a state of nature, and, if we insist on being left alone, we must show some evidence to the larger society that the children in our care are getting what we claim to be giving. We believe we can demonstrate that our system works through standardized tests, through the evaluation procedures that we and others offer under the auspices of the Regents, and through the performance of our graduates in institutions of higher learning and the working world. Our schools are open to observation and want to share their expertise and programs with any who care to partake. What we cannot accept is being asked to change what we do in the name of some lofty generality about what is good for all children.

We come to this conference this year with no special agenda, no list of monetary or other needs. What we seek always is the liberty, not the license, to do with our schools, in the service of the families we serve, what we think best, subject to evaluation by responsible peers and open to the wisdom of the rest of the educational community. In that way only can we preserve and protect for all our schools and colleges the right to be different.

THE PERSISTENCE
OF PRIVATE SCHOOLS

Bulletin 167, April 1992[1]

My assignment this afternoon is to get you to focus for a little while on private education in New York, understanding fully that the massive challenges of public education must always occupy the bulk of your time. Nevertheless, it is important (and to us vitally important) to remember that 477,000 New York children are being educated in 2,200 separate private schools and that those young people represent nearly 16% of all school-age students in the state. It's important to know also the magnitude of the economic impact of those educational enterprises on the polity and society of our state. The combined budgets of the 140 schools in my own association, for example, far exceed half a billion dollars, and we can assume that the combined expenditures of 2,200 schools must amount to several billion dollars per year with payrolls of tens of thousands of teaching and other staff. In brief, private education is a big business in New York State.

And it is also persistent. Our oldest school, we believe, is the Collegiate School, founded in 1628 in New Amsterdam. Collegiate has come through the Dutch hegemony, British imperialism, the American Revolution, Boss Tweed, and even Mayor Koch, and it's still here to tell the tale. Needless to say, an unsubsidized school does not survive for 364 years unless it is producing something that somebody wants. Against all odds, hundreds of private schools open their doors each fall with resources that would be laughable if those working as teachers and administrators were not in truth responding to a calling. Talk about persistence. All private schools must seek tuition each year from hundreds of thousands of parents who are already paying their full share of income, sales, and real-estate taxes that support schools to which they do not send their children. Under the circumstances, we can conclude that these are parents with a great deal of conviction.

So what are the contributions of the private schools other than being a big business? First, they are an alternative, in Regent Willard Genrich's words, to the public-school monolith. That's good for the monolith, and that's good for us. We both need competition. Second, private schools provide the only way to combine religious life and faith with general education. And, not surprisingly, most private schools are religiously based. Third, private schools allow small, manageable communities to construct a system of education that embodies their values and standards (often but not always religious in nature) and that is directly accountable to them. Fourth, in a fascinating contradiction to the much vaunted goals of diversity, private schools provide a way for our smallest minorities to gain a foothold and begin their entry into polyglot America. For example, the number of our Islamic schools has doubled since 1986. And last, private-school students continue to perform at above average levels, in part because of our ability to select them, but, we insist, in part because of the nature of our institutions, which are independent grass-roots communities responsible directly to their patrons.

In closing, I want to say how much more comfortable we in private education have felt in recent years with the new vision and attendant policies of the Board of Regents, the commissioner, and the State Education Department. Somehow the historic tension between the public and private sectors seems to have eased, and in one complicated undertaking after another we have worked constructively and reciprocally with the SED in ways we believe have been beneficial to us both. This happy state of affairs has not always been so, but the events of the last four and a half years have proved that it is possible to acknowledge the state's legitimate interest in the educational welfare of all its students without surrendering the independence we require to reach our goals. Although we are by nature and will always be suspicious, who said government was bad?

1. Excerpts from executive director's remarks to the New York State Board of Regents, February 20, 1992.

HOW ARE INDEPENDENT SCHOOLS DIFFERENT?

Bulletin 127, April 1988

If they are to serve their public purpose, which is to afford choice in education, independent schools must be free to be different. The differences that must be sustained and fostered are their independent control and individual philosophies; their unique educational programs, faculties, and student bodies; their fundamentally private financing; and their primary accountability to their clients.

Independent schools are particular rather than inclusive. They are designed to serve a particular constituency, which may be characterized by academic ability, by special interests, by special needs, or by the fact the students reside at the school. Independent schools develop programs appropriate to their particular constituencies, and employ teachers best suited to their particular purpose.

Independent schools are financed almost exclusively by private rather than public funds. They are directly and continuously accountable to students' parents. Those independent schools that do not satisfy the parents become extinct through a process of natural selection, when children are withdrawn and, along with them, the financial lifeblood on which the schools depend.

Independent schools also are different in that independent-school teachers interact with their students not only as instructors but as counselors, coaches, and directors in all aspects of social life. They are different in that curriculum is faculty-determined; teachers are accorded great freedom to teach in individual styles and to choose materials they deem appropriate to the particular students they teach; and parents play an active part in the governance of the school, choosing trustees and through trustees the school head.

Independent schools are not comprehensive schools but are rather designed for the designated elements in the community, be they the gifted, middle-of-the-road, learning disabled, verbally oriented, or visually oriented or those with special academic bents. They are able to respond readily to changing conditions and so can serve learners of different styles. And though, as with all human institutions, they are not immune to inertia, their relative freedom of action allows them to respond quickly and flexibly to societal changes and educational breakthroughs.

THE CONUNDRUM
OF DIVERSITY

Bulletin 156, March 1991

One of the vexing questions of our time is how diversity fits into
the unique context of private education in America. For, unlike
other sectors of our society, such as business and industry, health
care, government, public education, or the military, where diversity is a goal, diversity in most private schools is not ipso facto a
goal. For example, many people do not realize that some 90% of
all private schools are religiously based and actively seek students
who are members of their particular denomination. Since many
denominations are by definition racially, socially, and ethnically
homogeneous, especially in local concentrations, the school population tends also to be uniform. In the case of gender, a substantial
number of private schools are single-sex, which means, of course,
that they are not open to half the human race.

In many ways the whole point of being private or independent is to be homogeneous, not heterogeneous, though being
independent also confers the right to choose as much diversity as
a school wants. As we jealously guard our independence, we proclaim the virtue of each of our schools being different from any
other, free to develop its own culture and to pursue its own educational mission. It is not surprising that the issue of independence
is often fought out in the arena of academic freedom.

Somehow then we have to integrate two paradoxes into our thinking about diversity. The first is a parochial one. While NYSAIS defends the right of its schools to be different, it also requires its members to be nondiscriminatory, at least so far as the law requires. In other words, a school cannot turn down a student because of his race, but it can turn down a Hispanic boy because he is not a girl or because he is not Jewish or Quaker.

The second paradox is that if all private schools sought diversity as a primary goal, they would eventually become indistinguishable from one another, which would largely negate their essential individuality. This is to say that the principal historical reason for the existence of most private schools is to be counter-diverse.

Finally, while we may believe deeply, even passionately, in a multicultural, sex-blind world, we have to understand that the mission of many NYSAIS schools, and most private schools, is in many ways antithetical to diversity in the educational setting. (How strange it is to hear public educators advocating homogeneous schools in Milwaukee and New York City.) But if unreserved respect for every person is at the heart of a successful multicultural society, it must extend to the exercise of choice by all of our colleagues in private education, who work with as much devotion and integrity as we do.

THE DISCRIMINATION ADVANTAGE

Bulletin 235, February 1999

Present trends in American education stress uniformity. To reach higher standards teachers and students take standardized tests, now in specified subject areas. The theory is that if you can't pass, you are "remediated," or is it "irradiated"? Though no one likes to talk about it, at some stage, if you can't be retrained, you're thrown to the wolves. In any event, one set of tests fits all, and deviation is impermissible. Not to put too fine a point on it, but the Orwellians are cheering.

To the core of their being, private schools are nonconforming. They are in the business of discrimination, which means, in its best sense, making fine distinctions. Obviously, they embrace public policy. They do not discriminate in terms of race or national origin, but in practically every other respect they do. In virtually every case the origins of private schools are rooted in distinction. For the point of being private is to enjoy the least restrictive environment possible, in which schools may shape the educational community that fits their deepest held beliefs and practices.

In late-twentieth-century America the range of discrimination is still remarkable. Private schools may serve one religious denomination exclusively. They may accept children solely on the basis of IQ, high or low. They may choose to educate only one sex. As a practical matter they may determine the composition of their community, rich or poor, socially prominent or unknown, white-collar or blue. With few exceptions the private school continues to decide who comes through the door and, just as important, what happens to them educationally when they get there. And that, of course, is the secret of their success.

What we have learned over hundreds of years is that the educational program must serve the peculiar needs and motivational character of the constituency, and only thus can we achieve the highest performance. Discrimination in the best sense allows the formation of an intentional community whose limited goals insure quality. Uniform standards imposed from any quarter destroy the precious individuality that permissible discrimination confers and ultimately guarantee mediocrity and the deadness of collective thinking. All of educational research in the modern era leads to the efficacy of making fine distinctions about each child. Such has been the ideal of independent education from time immemorial.

INDEPENDENT SCHOOLS AND THE FREE MARKET

Bulletin 267, April 2002

Essentially, independent schools in America can do anything they want within the norms of ethical human conduct. They may discriminate in innumerable ways, for example, academically, religiously, socially, behaviorally, so long as they do not violate public policy. They may choose to educate boys or girls only. They may recruit athletes, xylophone players, or rising Michelangelos to their hearts' content. They may offer the strictest, most traditional curriculum, or, as does an alternative school in New England, let the students decide each day what they feel like doing. Schools are in theory, and often in practice, exemplars of the free market in education.

The idea of the free market in this case is that the best service wins, or more generously, the best services win. Most Americans like the free market in its most pleasant form. Its darker side, of course, is another issue. For independent schools, freedom to do or be what they want is restrained by only two external forces (other than legal curbs): the satisfaction of customers and peer pressure. The first is obvious and is at the core of our success. Independent schools have to produce the educational quality and style that their customers demand, or they go out of business. It's an ancient formula called direct accountability to the consumer. The second, peer pressure, is more subtle and less powerful, but still a force to be reckoned with.

Peer pressure is strongest among independent schools where there are large aggregations in and around cities. To stop what some consider predatory practices, agreements (a type of treaty) are reached in admissions including common reply dates, limits on recruiting, and respect for signed enrollment contracts. Understandings about hiring are also observed, including restrictions on poaching, proper notification, and open communication. In some cases, attempts are made to curb recruitment of athletes to avoid the interscholastic absurdity of one school being overwhelmingly dominant in a specific sport. Taken together, such practices prevent jungle warfare, and the penalty for the nonconformist is ostracism.

But what if independent schools, within societal limits, engaged, as it were, in an unrestrained Adam Smith play? The free-market purists contend that ultimately students and families would be best served. Schools would struggle prodigiously to meet customer needs, to eliminate outdated programs, to manage efficiently, and to resist educational inertia. The strongest, best-run schools in their sphere would survive and flourish. Others that could not compete in the marketplace would expire, leading, the purists say, to overall higher quality. Endless commercial parallels could be cited, from the impact of the Japanese on the American automobile industry to the triumph of United States technology in the world marketplace. But as with all pure plays, there are downsides that usually have to do with issues of humaneness, nonviolence, and the survival, not of the institutions themselves, but of the people who compose them.

The actuality of the independent-school world is that the free-market system generally prevails with a few but important constraints. First, the state requires certain minimum standards, largely in the realms of health and safety. Public policy also forbids racial and ethnic discrimination and several other practices in matters of employment. Bullies in the marketplace are held in check either by local compacts or codes of good behavior promulgated by state and national associations. The accrediting process, to which most schools adhere, can also modify the conduct of market mavericks. But otherwise, though some might last longer than in a totally free market, independent schools have to perform to survive and certainly to flourish. Among NYSAIS members alone, fourteen schools have either closed or merged since 1988, while at least an equal number have started up or come of age. For those that left the scene, it's a sad story; for the enterprise of private education, however, there is indisputably a healthy form of Darwinism at work.

THE MEANING OF ASSOCIATION

Bulletin 294, December 2004

Though independent to their core, NYSAIS member schools, now numbering 170, have to function together. Most are in relatively close proximity to each other (there are 68 on the island of Manhattan), and only a few are truly isolated. Associations like NYSAIS exist in the wake of Ben Franklin's warning that we either hang together or we hang alone. Founded in 1947 by a band of brothers and sisters who fought the State Education Department in its attempt to license all private schools, we eventually won our case, *Packer Collegiate Institute v. University of the State of New York*, in New York's Court of Appeals. That decision—together with *Dartmouth College v. Woodward* and *Pierce v. the Society of Sisters* in the United States Supreme Court—constitutes the bedrock on which our independence rests.[1]

Despite such legal precedents, never to be taken lightly, we know that nothing is permanent. Each generation must defend its principles. Today NYSAIS schools stand firmly on the issue of "required" high-stakes testing, believing that education, in its essence, is not training. Your association maintains a substantial reserve fund for the day when forces from any quarter challenge what we believe to be our rights. There is no doubt that once again our schools will band together in the face of mindless or arbitrary intervention from any source. For it is in the end our freedom to construe our educational programs as we see fit, always, of course, respecting the needs and opinions of our communities. The key to the whole enterprise is accountability (still sadly absent from the public monolith), which stands so simply on the premise of reward for service.

The strength of NYSAIS relies also on standards that we can exhibit confidently to the outside world. For these we maintain a rigorous system of evaluation and accreditation conducted by peers, not bureaucrats. Some would argue cynically that evaluation by peers is in its nature self-serving. But if peers are serious people (if they are not, then everything we do is fraudulent), they know that self-preservation lies not in concealing friends' weaknesses but in impelling them to grow stronger. While there is no legal basis for accreditation in New York State, the designation is nevertheless a badge of excellence, never a perfect measure of any one school's qualities but an honest and careful one. Whatever the flaws, schools that have accreditation don't want to lose it, and those that don't have it want it.

While NYSAIS does not publish a comprehensive code of ethics, except for admissions and hiring guidelines, there is a commonly held sense of good practice among and between schools. Generally, NYSAIS schools keep their promises to students, staff, patrons, outside organizations, and the public. They are, in a word, honorable institutions. Our schools do not mislead about their missions, conditions, or capabilities. They do not poach either students or personnel. And they protect confidentiality in all its manifestations, when the welfare of students and parents is at stake. In the final analysis the good practice of our schools rests in the understanding and mutual respect of our heads. For it is they who ultimately set the standard and have the courage when necessary to acknowledge failings and correct course. That our schools as a group are enormously strengthened by what is at bottom moral leadership is beyond debate. Let it never subside.

1. See "The Roots of Independence," pp. 21–25.

INTERPRETING NYSAIS GUIDELINES

Bulletin 135, February 1989

Several months ago NYSAIS published its "Trustee Guidelines of Good Practice for Schools." The guidelines try to address ethical and procedural issues in admissions and hiring, two areas that arouse competitive instincts. Although nearly everyone favors high ethical standards in theory, two factors in our contemporary world make it harder to observe them in practice. One is the fact that our goals for institutional behavior far exceed what goes on in most of our society, and we are thus surrounded by the worst kind of modeling. The other is that when issues of survival are at stake, ethics have a way of giving ground.

For example, NYSAIS guidelines do not intend to imply that there is anything unethical about aggressive marketing per se. The issue is joined only when aggressive marketing veers into negative campaigning, i.e., when a school stops talking about its own strengths and advantages and starts talking about a competitor's weaknesses and disadvantages. By the same token, NYSAIS guidelines frown on marketing efforts that are personally directed to named students in a competitor school either via the mail, by phone, or through face-to-face contact. Therefore, the guidelines for admissions are designed not to protect sleepy schools from the consequences of their slumber, but to protect all schools from the consequences of cut-throat competition.

In the hiring realm NYSAIS also goes well beyond common practice in the corporate and public spheres. Some may think us naïve, but we urge our schools to support their employees' ambitions for advancement, believing that an atmosphere of openness and honesty produces a healthier, happier school. The guidelines frown on forcing a teacher to break a contract at one school in order to move to another. They abjure secret recruiting of talent without informing the authorities of the targeted school. Yet they recognize also a teacher's right to explore opportunities elsewhere in confidence until matters become serious, at which time they require the respective schools to communicate. Ultimately, the Trustee Guidelines of Good Practice try to ensure the integrity of all NYSAIS schools, in the belief that the only real value of independence is to exceed the standards of the lowest common denominator. If that makes us ethical dinosaurs, we are proud of the designation.

POLITICS AND EDUCATION

INTRODUCTION

When I asked George Pataki to define "good politics," he replied, "Good politics is when you and I disagree about the solution to a problem, but we both believe that our solution benefits the people in a meaningful way." Fred Calder and his writings exemplify Governor Pataki's concept of good politics. Though a Quaker, Fred rarely ducks an argument if he feels the well-being of our independent schools might be threatened. Over the course of Fred's twenty years at the helm of the New York State Association of Independent Schools, the state and its empowered leaders have sought to impress upon our schools burdensome regulations without any clear benefit to our task at hand, which is to educate young people.

Fred voiced his dissent about the Regents' Action Plan proposed for private schools in the mid-1980s as if the future of every independent school of the land rested on this challenge. Just as Daniel Webster in 1818 argued before the Supreme Court in defense of Dartmouth College's right of independence, "It is, Sir, as I have said, a small college. And yet, there are those who love it," Fred has fought for our autonomy with vigor, and has championed the belief that "the best education is that which grows from the unfettered commitment, insight, and devotion of small communities."[1] To hear Fred testify before a State Senate committee or a group of Regents is to understand how he balances his pacifist heritage with his firm belief in independence.

More recently, the high-stakes testing initiated under Thomas Sobol (formerly the state's commissioner of education) again challenged our sense of independence. Fred, always an ardent supporter of both the little guy and the breadth of the schools that he represents, refused to surrender to the one-size-fits-all mentality of the required exams. He firmly believes that we do our job best by being left alone to do it well. Perhaps behind the testing movement was an attempt by the politicos to find a way to measure schools in the hopes of improving or closing those that are weak. Fred reminded whoever would listen that our accreditation process and parental evaluation are more than sufficient indicators of a school's success. Students and parents have a choice, and they can and will vote with their feet.

Having taken on the Board of Regents of New York, Fred was emboldened to challenge national magazines and their so-called rankings of universities and independent schools. How can independent schools be compared and ranked, he argued, if by their very design they are as different from one another as they are the same? If the education provided by our schools is equal to or better than that offered by the public sector, freedom from state regulations encourages individual schools to design their curricula to serve specific populations in the best way they see fit.

All these issues center on our schools' single core belief: independence. Since we exist to do what we believe prudent, we should be free from the restrictions placed upon us by well-intentioned people who seek to codify our schools. If we are truly independent, then we must hold our destiny in our own hands, for good or bad. Fred has frequently reminded us that schools never fail because of bad teaching; they fail because of bad leadership. We remain strong because Fred has championed our cause, while simultaneously pushing each school to abide by and even excel in its unique mission.

ARCHIBALD A. SMITH III
Headmaster, Trinity-Pawling School

1. From "For and Against," p. 67.

THE JOYS AND SORROWS OF CHOICE

Bulletin 158, May 1991

The current rage in education is *choice*. In a country built on the ideal of free choice how could anyone oppose it? But the unions and public-school boards and many others do. They say that choice of schools by parents, particularly subsidized choice of private schools, would introduce chaos and fatally weaken the public schools. What they do not say but think is that those now in control would be displaced, and power and perquisites thrown to the winds.

Except in a few experimental pockets (such as Milwaukee and Minnesota), choice has been largely a theoretical exercise. But President George H. W. Bush's recent promulgation of "America 2000: An Education Strategy" and a suddenly resurrected Department of Education have changed the equation. Now choice, while still many battles away, could conceivably take hold in significant parts of the nation.

At first blush, choice for private schools would seem a godsend. At long last parents could tap the state for funds to help pay tuition. The forces of competition, already embedded in private education, would thrive as never before. All of education would profit.

But the origins of choice are not private-school origins. The overriding societal purpose of choice is to strengthen public schools. The president does not advocate choice to enhance Phillips Andover or Happy Valley Day School. The nightmare of an apparatus of choice for most politicians and the public-school establishment would be greatly strengthened private schools and a slightly improved public system. We may be sure that no one is going to let that happen.

Clearly, if choice comes, it must embody some version of the voucher system. Direct state subsidies could not survive the First Amendment, and even the nonsectarians would be insane to accept them. Yet even a voucher approach does not exclude regulation, which is, of course, our own abiding bad dream. Nothing as important as the concept of choice should be dismissed, but private-school people had better proceed carefully with the Homeric warning firmly in mind.

CHOICE AND THE FIRST AMENDMENT

Bulletin 176, March 1993

Although the Clinton administration seems anything but friendly toward educational choice (government subsidies to parents to be spent as they wish for their children's education), the idea does not go away. Continuing frustration with public schools in many places keeps the concept alive. And the growing understanding that a postmodern economy cannot tolerate an untrained labor force is finally awakening Americans to the primacy of education for the future of our country.

What is interesting about this whole raging debate is that we wouldn't even be discussing educational choice today if it were not for one clause in the First Amendment, namely, "Congress shall make no law respecting an establishment of religion." Whatever the Founding Fathers' intent may have been, the establishment clause has come to mean that government, essentially, may not grant money to any church or church-affiliated activity, period. And since 85% of private schools are religiously based, the prohibition of direct state aid has been effectively applied to all private schools, religious and nonsectarian alike. Whether we agree or not with the courts' view of the establishment clause, the cost of the First Amendment to the American educational system has yet to be measured.

To put all of this in perspective, it is important to point out that the United States is virtually the only developed democratic nation in which it is not routine to subsidize all private schools.

In Australia, for example, where 30% of children attend private schools, government subsidies range from 20% of the budget for a comparatively wealthy independent school to 100% for certain aboriginal schools that are still technically private. Catholic schools, which constitute by far the largest number of private schools, collect up to 80% of their operating funds from the state. Unlike the Catholic school system here, which has suffered grievous shrinkage in recent years (at exactly the time it is most needed), its counterpart in Australia is flourishing.

It's easy to understand why people who are hostile to private education are such fervent supporters of the establishment clause. They know that a large and healthy private system, as in Australia, requires government aid. It's harder to understand why so many people who believe in private schools are equally committed to the First Amendment prohibition. For without access to tax dollars in the long run, the 12% of American children now educated in private schools may well become 9% or 6%, and there will be, in Regent Willard Genrich's words, no alternative to the monolith. Clearly, as long as our schools stand alone, devoid of public funds, we should resist state regulation unswervingly. But we should also think long and carefully about the peculiar tradition that forces so many American parents to pay billions of dollars in school taxes, none of which benefit the education of their children.

CHOICE AGAIN

Bulletin 302, October 2005

More than a decade ago the NYSAIS Board of Trustees embraced the concept of income-tax credits, and to a lesser extent, vouchers, to help economically excluded families gain access to private education. The National Association of Independent Schools also went on record in support of such programs. Obviously, people in the upper income brackets have essentially unlimited choice about how and where to educate their children. Independent schools could not exist without the patronage of this core group. But lower-income families have little or no choice, stuck as they are in housing patterns that dictate public-school attendance and unable to obtain financial aid from limited private-school budgets. The fundamental argument for government support of families who want choice is that *all* citizens are subject to income, real-estate, and sales taxes that pay for public schools, but are unable to direct any of those funds to private schooling, if they so wish. As more and more Americans become disillusioned with public schools, the basic unfairness of the present system demands redress.

Originally, the idea of income-tax credits related to the personal expense of parents for the education of their child. That is, a $1,000 tax credit could be taken for one's child with the submission of a receipt for tuition paid to an approved private school. Since then the concept has evolved from the personal expense approach to what is called the donation tax credit. In the state of

Arizona, for example, any person may give up to $500 to an approved 501(c)(3) Scholarship Granting Organization (there are now fifty-five SGOs) and take a credit against his or her state income tax. Any additional amount may be taken as a deduction on federal taxes as well. The SGO then distributes "financial aid" to students in private schools according to criteria that are themselves evolving. The Arizona program is now seven years old and has been approved by the courts. In 2004 $32 million was donated, and 21,000 students are being served. The state has imposed no additional regulations on private schools in connection with the tax-credit scheme. Pennsylvania is in the fourth year of a program similar except that donations must come from corporations, not individuals. Thus far 20,000 students are receiving aid from 150 SGOs.

We know, of course, that in our far-flung country New York is a long way from Arizona, and that even Pennsylvania's culture is different in many ways from New York's. But the New York State Coalition of Independent and Religious Schools believes that the moment has come to mount a serious and sustained campaign to introduce donation tax credits to New York. The immediate goal is to raise $500,000 to fund advocacy organizations and political action committees that can compete with groups, such as school board associations and unions, that oppose tax credits on principle. For far too long the New York State legislature has heard one side of the story and accepted donations from those who at all costs want to protect the public-school establishment from having to compete with their independent brethren. NYSAIS, as the central organization for independent schools in New York, finally has an opportunity to promote and develop with its colleagues a program for real parental choice in education that actually has a chance of succeeding. No one thinks this will be easy. However, with successful models in place around the country and with the political will to spend resources and energy, there are signs that the time is indeed ripe.

INTERESTING TIMES

Bulletin 246, March 2000

As the debate over standards, accountability, and school choice rages throughout the country, it may be said that we in education live in interesting times. If the outcome were not so important, the resolution of these issues could even be said to be fun. In the presidential debate between Bradley and Gore conducted in Harlem last month, a questioner from the floor asked Gore how he could be against choice (that is, vouchers or tax credits) and send his children to prestigious private schools. The vice president did not answer except to say that he supports public schools and does not wish to drain resources from them. But the question still stands. The rich enjoy educational choice; the poor, generally, do not.

Last week a serious person in the educational world was heard to say that he was impressed with the new New York City schools chancellor, because he was "totally committed to public education." Someone asked how that could be since the chancellor sends his children to an independent school. Is it possible to be "somewhat" committed or "partially" committed, and, if so, what does that mean? The truth is that everyone in the United States is forced to support public education through the payment of taxes, which are indiscriminately visited on users and nonusers alike. Theoretically, you could go to jail for refusing to pay those taxes. Some people pay for public schools gladly; others under duress, feeling that the service of education is *not* best supplied by monopolistic government.

If pressed, what indeed would the vice president or New York chancellor say to the issue of public assertions versus private behavior? The answer must be: "The independent school is better for my child." This situation is not unlike the African American parent whose child attends a Catholic school in Florida on vouchers. If the vouchers were to go, she said she would give up cable, disconnect her phone, and get a night job to keep her daughter in the school. And if that's not total commitment, what is? The point is that we must never be apologetic about these realities.

It's interesting that the more conservative political party in this political year advocates the radical idea of vouchers, and the more liberal party is against them. Why is that? For heaven's sake, as the debate about schooling in America heats up, let's at least start telling the truth.

CENTRAL PLANNING
VERSUS LOCAL INITIATIVE

Bulletin 128, May 1998

The Regents' Action Plan, part 100, of recent years essentially imposed curriculum requirements on all New York State schools. The entire procedure was a case of central planners, armed with the authority of government, writing an educational prescription for all to swallow. For some, it was too big a pill. NYSAIS, among others, managed to negotiate a system of variances that freed its schools of the more onerous aspects of the plan.[1]

Much of the unhappiness with the Regents' Action Plan stems from its major theoretical premise: that effective reform can be achieved by dictation from the top. Independent schools believe in the intrinsic worth of every person—teachers, students, parents—and that each has an appropriate contribution to make to the educational process. The educational program is, therefore, a collaborative undertaking led by teachers with the consent of students and parents, and made vibrant by the high expectations that each partner places upon the other.

How refreshing after the autocratic certainty of the Action Plan to have the Report of the Commissioner's Task Force on the Teaching Profession of March 1988 (despite the absence of a single nonpublic-school representative). "We are calling," says the document, "for schools that are centered on the learner and operated through joint decision-making, allowing teachers—those closest to the children's educational needs—a real voice in determining their students' education. Teachers would be treated as the professionals they are."

Can it be that the Regents will soon be considering recommendations that reject the prescriptive approach to education so recently visited upon us, and that restore initiative to the practitioners who deliver our cultural heritage each day to their students? What a radical concept! What a blessed event for New York State and all its children!

1. The Regents' Action Plan stemmed from the Regents' Goals for Elementary and Secondary School Students (1984). Part 100 of the plan included a provision for a series of tests to be administered in all schools in New York State. NYSAIS developed, with the commissioner of education, a permanent variance procedure. Participating NYSAIS schools would agree to show evidence of program and student accomplishment that substantially satisfied the Regents' Goals, and would be free of the obligation to administer New York State tests whose content or level were either tangential to individual schools' programs or insufficiently demanding of their students.

DINNER WITH
THE REGENTS

Bulletin 137, April 1989

For the first time in eight years the New York State Regents invited representatives of the "nonpublic" schools to dinner at the New York State Museum in Albany on April 13. Attendees included Catholics, Jews, Lutherans, Seventh Day Adventists, and Christians. Representing NYSAIS was Gardner Dunnan, vice president, and yours truly. Commissioner of Education Thomas Sobol, numerous deputy and assistant commissioners, and other department members also attended. Nearly all of the sixteen Regents were present.

While all such occasions are pleasant enough, this one seemed particularly congenial. Several of us were asked to speak and, from subsequent comments and interlocutions, the Regents seemed to be listening carefully. Speaking for the New York State Coalition for Nonpublic Education and for NYSAIS, I said in part:

Turning to the issue of local accountability, we are very much aware of the Regents' and the department's recent efforts to encourage all schools in New York State not only to meet minimum standards but to aspire to educational excellence. We applaud that effort and are aware of the department's plan for public-school accountability, which the Regents will consider in the near future.

Obviously, it is not our business as institutions to tell the public schools how to do their job, and, by the same logic, it is not the business of the public sector to tell us how to meet our responsibilities as educational institutions. Nor is it appropriate or useful to generalize from the public-school experience, or the needs of public schools, when determining what the private schools should be doing or not doing.

For to be independent is by definition to be accountable, since every single student who enters one of our schools, or chooses to stay, does so by virtue of his or his parents' free choice. And that choice, it is important to remember, involves the payment from discretionary net income of often substantial tuition and fees, *after* having paid both real-estate taxes and state income taxes for the support of public schools. The point is that the decision to send a child to an independent school is both serious and costly, and that to win the support of the families we serve independent schools have to perform! There is no captive audience.

Accountability in the private schools is built in at all levels. First, and most crucially, is the parents' freedom to withdraw a child at any time whatsoever and transfer him or her to another private school or to a "nonprivate" school. Second, in virtually all private schools, parents are heavily involved in shaping educational priorities through parents' associations, serving on governing boards, in some cases electing trustees, and generally feeling free to collar administrators and teachers in classrooms, in corridors, in parking lots, and at home on the telephone. Third, in most private schools teachers are major participants in policy-making and *are* the dominant influence in curriculum development and planning. Finally, virtually all private-school personnel at the administrative level— and, for that matter, thousands of our teachers—are reviewed and rehired *annually*. There is very little institutionalized job security.

So what is the state's interest in local accountability among the nonpublic schools? Not very much, it would appear, since the conditions for local accountability already exist in abundance within our schools. As it is, the private schools supply the State Education Department annually with powerful evidence of school performance, including results of state tests or other standardized tests, drop-out rates, enrollment data, attendance records, and high-school and graduate profiles. Our schools strongly agree with current thinking in the department that local planning for educational excellence is an integral component of effective schools. We assert that evidence of such planning (which one of the schools in my association has been doing since 1628) is reflected in student achievement, and is regularly made available to each school's governing board and to its local school community.

A CLASHING OF CYMBALS

Bulletin 147, April 1990

It may sound like cymbals, but most of what is going on in Albany this month as governor and legislature forge a budget is the clashing of symbols. What we will never quite know is whether all the sound and fury truly serve the commonweal or whether this is at root a time-honored strategy that merely serves the politics of incumbency. Whatever it is, it demeans representative government, diminishes our respect for the political process, and generally promotes cynicism at the expense of faith.

How do independent schools relate to all of this? Notwithstanding the personal income-tax cuts of recent years, the aggregate state and local taxes that New Yorkers pay are among the highest, if not the highest, in the nation. This means, presumably, that New Yorkers have fewer net dollars than most other United States citizens to spend on private education. It means that state aid for textbooks, library materials, and science equipment that directly affects students will at best be frozen for another year. It means that new state funding to help defray the nonpublic schools' bill of $98 million for asbestos removal will be either pitifully inadequate or absent altogether. And it means that other new taxes, on gasoline, long-distance telephone calls, or whatever the politicians concoct, will in some way increase the cost of operating private schools.

Several years ago the Regents' Action Plan decreed that all high-school curricula must have a government component, apparently to assure that the state's young people be schooled in the principles and practice of good government. As we watch once again the April spectacle of rampant partisanship and self-serving politicking in Albany, it is tragically clear that if our young people don't do something about it, no one will. Certainly, their elders are demonstrating every day that under the current circumstances of American politics, they seem helpless to rise to a level of statesmanship that New York desperately needs.

THE CHARTER SCHOOL MESS

Bulletin 266, March 2002

It was inevitable that someone in authority would eventually challenge the existence of charter schools in New York. In this case, two state legislators have called for a two-year moratorium on the issuance of charters for new schools. In December 1999 the New York State Legislature reluctantly agreed to allow the creation of up to two hundred charter schools (thirty-two have actually materialized), if the governor would sign a bill raising members' salaries. The usual groups, of course, opposed the establishment of charter schools, and raising legislative salaries is always a hard sell. Aside from the virtues of either issue, however, the whole episode was another lovely example of how state government works in New York.

The chances of charter schools succeeding in New York State are slim at best for a number of reasons. First, they are detested by the public-school establishment, namely, superintendents and other administrators, boards of education, and the unions, primarily because they consume public funds without being subject to the establishment's direct control. The whole point of charter schools, notwithstanding, is to provide alternatives to families who are not being served by the monolith, something private-school people understand. Theoretically, as children switch from a public school to a charter school, the cost of educating them goes with them. For example, if there were a charter school educating three hundred of a district's students, the local system's schools should be able to cut expenses accordingly, while the charter gets the dollars thus saved. Makes sense, doesn't it? Or does it?

Second, the legislation allowing charter schools failed (some think intentionally) to include funds for physical facilities. Thus schools are forced to beg, scrounge, or conduct fund-raising campaigns, while trying to get an embryonic institution to start breathing. Third, while charter schools enjoy a degree of independence in their governance, hiring practices, and so on, they are required to choose their student applicants by lot. The result is that a school with a specialized mission has to deal with students ranging from seriously disabled to gifted. And as with all "public" schools, charters cannot easily dismiss students who are disruptive or simply unable to cope academically.

Finally, charters tend to be theme schools in the sense that they are founded by groups of people who wish to promote certain educational philosophies or methodologies. For example, a charter school may emphasize the arts or sciences or may commit to a highly regimented style. In the beginning there is enormous enthusiasm and energy as a new idea takes hold and hope outpaces reality. After a few years or less, exhaustion sets in, as the founders discover that running a school under any circumstances, but especially those of the charters, is a prodigiously hard job. Without the freedom, the resources, the management skills, and at least the neutrality of the establishment, the prospects for survival are bleak. Already, some charter schools have closed around the country, and until the environment and other conditions change, more probably will.

Sadly, the story of charter schools is the story of the politicization of American public education. The concept of charter schools is a noble one. Let small aggregations of people invent and control their schools for the benefit of their children. Let their schools be accountable to their patrons, not to bureaucracy and democratic politics. And let them be funded disinterestedly by the state with monies saved by attrition from the public system. Is this a joke or just a modest proposal doomed to suffer and expire? Whatever it

is, we mourn for the children who stay stuck by the tens of thousands in the politics of education in America. And we work even
harder to preserve and protect the idea and practice of independent schooling as we know it.

FOR AND AGAINST

Bulletin 305, February 2006

For years most of NYSAIS's political work in Albany has focused on minimizing government interference in our schools. From the Regents'Action Plan of the mid-1980s to local accountability under Commissioner Thomas Sobol to high-stakes testing of the last decade, NYSAIS has striven to protect our schools' independence. In that sense our attitude toward government has been generally negative. We tend to be against state initiatives, regulatory or legislative, that restrict our freedom of action. But, lest we be accused of grumpy philistinism, the truth is that being *against* state intrusion, in this case, means that we are *for* something much more important. And that is our unswerving belief that the best education is that which grows from the unfettered commitment, insight, and devotion of small communities. That being said, it is nevertheless a pleasure in 2006 to support enthusiastically with all of our private-school comrades a new government program that could have profound implications for the children of New York State.

At this writing, following a press conference and rally that brought thousands of people to the steps of the state capitol, it appears that some form of tuition tax credit could actually become law in New York State. Several states, including Arizona and Pennsylvania, have had tax-credit programs in place for a number of years. What tax credits mean is that individuals or corporations, as the case may be, may take a credit, not a deduction, against their state income tax for some portion of funds designated for students' tuition. Although methods vary, the bottom line is that state monies raised through taxation help subsidize indirectly tuition payments to private schools. Tax credits, of course, have been used for decades to promote certain behaviors, for example, for energy conservation or the purchase of hybrid cars. This time they're for education.

The case for tuition tax credits rests on moral and practical grounds. First, those who believe, as NYSAIS does, in parental choice, enshrined in the great Supreme Court case *Pierce v. the Society of Sisters* of 1925, understand that true choice exists only for upper-income families. Tax credits at least begin to afford real choice for lower-income families who are condemned to underperforming schools. The possibility of transforming the educational prospects of able children stuck in poverty is more than inspiring. Second, if parental choice is a moral and legal right in America, why should not some portion of school taxes paid by every adult citizen be available for private education? The United States is, after all, the only developed country in the world that does not subsidize nonpublic schools. Third, a firmly established tax-credit system would allow NYSAIS schools one of two options: either to expand financial-aid budgets by the amount of tax-credit benefits they receive or to reduce financial aid proportionately to relieve the school of unsustainable costs. Either way, it's a good outcome.

Clearly, most NYSAIS schools would never accept tuition tax credits if their independence were threatened in any way. Thus far, in states where tax credits are established, no state regulation has followed. Since schools do not receive state funds in any form through tax credits, it's difficult to see how governments could equate regulation with such a program. Needless to say, everyone connected with the tax-credit movement is more than alert to these issues. Whatever happens, we can be assured that the story will unfold.

MERIT VERSUS POLITICS

Bulletin 307, April 2006

Let me try to explain. New York's governor for the first time in history included tuition tax credits in his executive budget early in the new year. Several other states are already well along with tuition tax credits, which are helping tens of thousands of children attend private schools. In other words, in the face of failing public schools lower-income parents actually have a chance to exercise educational choice as upper-income parents have always been able to do. Parenthetically, the governor's proposal in New York would also allow tax credits to be used for tutoring and other educational services regardless of private-school enrollment.

Support for the governor's idea has been remarkable. The New York State Coalition for Independent and Religious Schools has led the charge. The building-trades union and others have joined in the effort. On February 14 a rally and press conference were held in the capital. Prominent members of the Assembly and Senate spoke powerfully in support. Cardinal Egan, standing with Governor Pataki on the steps of the capitol, addressed thousands of adults and students who had come from the far corners of the state. Emails and postcards poured into the legislature. It was an impressive display of enthusiasm for an idea whose time has come.

But then the New York State teachers union decided to call in its chits. Enormous pressure was applied to legislators to defeat the proposal. The union has always maintained, despite the logical fallacy, that tax credits or vouchers drain money from the public schools and thus weaken them. Does it not follow that if, say, fifty thousand students are going to private schools, the public schools have fifty thousand less to educate and pay for? What we are really talking about, of course, is a perceived loss of power, and that is enough to generate the wildest assertions of irresponsibility.

The outcome was the passage of a "child tax credit," which would be granted to the parents of children aged four to seventeen within certain income limits simply as a reward for the act of procreation. The credit would be unrelated to education, though it could be used theoretically to help pay tuition. It could also be used to buy pizza. The absurdity and essential immorality of such a tax credit stun the imagination. One wonders what it would actually take to embarrass our legislative leaders, who supposedly represent the best interests of the republic.

At this writing, the governor, not surprisingly, has vetoed the child tax credit. A number of things could happen. The veto could be overridden, but might then face court challenges. A compromise could be reached, saving faces all around, though one shudders to think what that might be. Or the whole idea could come crashing down for now. The good news is that a year ago no one could have foreseen getting this far in New York. Further those who believe in the rightness and efficacy of parental choice through tax credits are determined to move ahead for the sake of innumerable children who need and deserve an alternative to what they have. It has been an honor for NYSAIS to be part of the struggle.

THE REALITY
OF ACCREDITATION

Bulletin 256, March 2001

One of the most misunderstood words in education may well be *accreditation*. Somehow the word has the ring of authority, and everyone seems to want it, if the cost is not too high. Some people think the state confers it, some think it has legal implications; others don't know where it comes from, but would rather have it than not. The fact is that the accreditation of a school is based on a system of standards impartially upheld by an association of peers. Its legitimacy rests solely on a common agreement among institutions of similar purpose that accreditation represents a measure of excellence. For better or worse, that's all it is.

The origins of accreditation could well reside in the ethic of medieval guilds in which artisans banded together to protect and promote their crafts. In time the guilds became symbols of accomplished skill, and to be a member was a recognition of high performance. It is no accident that our forebears in New York City chose to call their local association the Guild of Independent Schools. Judgment by peers is an ancient and honorable concept with deep roots in British jurisprudence. Critics, of course, assert that peers are the worst judges, because they will too often forgive the failings of their brothers and sisters. But the countervailing argument, which has stood the test of time, is that the survival of the peer group requires unshakable integrity.

Thus, for the sake of the whole, malpractice by even a few may not be allowed.

As the tempests of standards-based testing rage through the country and the schools become targets of opportunity, the issue of accreditation enters the public realm. What does it signify? Does it measure quality? Who sanctions it? Who cares? The State of New York, for example, has never recognized accreditation as a valid representation of anything. At best, the state's view seems to be, "It can't hurt." Instead, private schools may seek voluntary registration, which requires a visit by one education official for a few hours every twenty years or so. Many public schools that have been accredited by a third-party agency for decades are dropping out of the process as New York imposes content-based examinations as a prerequisite for a diploma. What's the point of accreditation, if nothing counts but training students to take prepackaged tests? If education is a lost cause, why waste time measuring its components?

The fate of independent schools is another question. As they defend themselves from the depredations of state testing in the name of curricular autonomy, original thinking, and high motivation teaching, they will need more than ever a credible, rigorous system of peer evaluation. The survival of independent schools, unlike government schools, depends at least as much on strong governance and fiscal management as it does on academic performance. The emblem of accreditation must signify the health and strength of the entire institution. If the day ever comes when we must once again defend our independence in the courts of law, a record of consistent, proven, comprehensive self-evaluation that can demonstrate school improvement over time will be part of the bedrock of our case. There is no easy way to evaluate a whole school. There are no shortcuts. Inexorably, the ten-year cycle comes around. But the experience of half a century keeps telling us that it's worth it.

VIVE LA DIFFERENCE

Bulletin 216, March 1997

Prolonged frustration with low performing schools has led to max-
imalist solutions. They take the form of "national standards,"
school report cards, and, in New York, Regents examinations for
all high-school students. Similar frustration with crime in America has led to longer prison sentences, limited parole, and less judicial
discretion. In a sense, national standards and all the rest put education in prison too. The more monolithic the system, the narrower
the choices. The high Federalists of the late eighteenth century,
against whom Thomas Jefferson relentlessly fought, would have
loved national standards. Virtue is served when enlightened politicians or bureaucrats decide what is good for us.

Unfortunately, maximalism appears to work, at least for a time.
If everyone teaches toward a single test, scores will generally rise.
The method and content of any test can be mastered with focused
training. Even the most modest students will get some of it. But
the question is not how well students do on required tests. The
question is what students *don't learn* in the broader spectrum of
human knowledge. National standards and state testing have elec-
toral implications. They must be made to work by hook or crook.
And, sad as it is, that means reducing complexity or limiting content. You can't flunk half the population.

Much too much of education reform is driven by misguided
egalitarianism. We see it in President Clinton's proposal for a $1,500

college-tuition tax credit. The drop-out rate in less competitive colleges is already immense. Why make it worse by subsidizing even more potential dropouts? Does it really make sense to say that *every* boy and girl should have a chance to go to college? Why are the politicians afraid to say every *qualified* boy and girl? When Jefferson wrote that "all men are created equal," he didn't mean intellectually, emotionally, and physically. He meant before the law. Even with its limitations then, that was a dizzyingly revolutionary concept.

The tragedy is that national standards, school report cards, and required state testing are fundamentally political undertakings. They try to dull the pain of pluralism, and they pervert the search for truth. By their very rigidity they convert the meaning of education from leading out to leading in, all for the sake of some delusional notion of equality. Those in the public schools who object to the standardization of education face a nearly hopeless task. Because, ultimately, the politicians and the ideologues have the money. How can public school *educators* stand up to the standardization juggernaut, when those at the helm pay their salaries? If ever there were an argument for private education, this is it.

The fight to preserve our schools from statist ideology probably has no end, only lulls. Our best defense is high performance within the mission of each school, and a credible, powerful system of evaluation and accreditation devoid of comradely back-scratching. One of the major distinctions between the contemporary public and independent schools is the former's commitment to an unachievable equality. Theoretically, every public-school student can do the same work and pass the Regents exams. Independent schools make no such claim. Our missions range from serving the high-powered academic to the learning disabled, our student bodies from brilliant to modest, our curricula from mainstream to offbeat. The whole point of independent education is the acceptance of differences. If we should ever surrender that conviction, our reason for being will have vanished.

TESTING AS EDUCATION

Bulletin 242, October 1999

The country is fixated on the efficacy of standardized tests. The presidential candidates proclaim them; even New York's Regents seem to have embraced them. The tests, they say, are the answer to abysmal student performance in failed schools. By the design of harder tests and teachers being held accountable, students will be goaded to perform better. And, best of all, politicians can claim victory for improving American education. The voices of those who know something about teaching and learning are stilled by the clamor of popular opinion. Clearly, it is a time to stay calm but firm until this too passes.

In independent schools, at least, standardized tests have a small but important part in the educational process. That is to take an occasional measurement for purposes of comparability or diagnosis. Schools need to know where they stand among peers or against national norms. Even the state has a legitimate interest in knowing whether the skills of private-school students are at least equivalent to those in the public schools. As for diagnosis, psychological and sophisticated skills tests can be enormously useful for identifying individual learning problems. No longer do we simply write off low performing students as lazy or stupid without investigation.

But standardized subject-area tests in English, mathematics, science, global studies, and American history as proposed by

New York State for all graduating students are anathema to our very reason for being. First, they deprive schools of their curricular autonomy, which is the whole point of being private. From the teaching of religious studies to the designation of course content, if we cannot design our programs according to our best lights and the needs of our communities, then let the monolith prevail and give up the enterprise of educating. Second, the foundation of our pedagogy is the idea of the Socratic method, which by its nature leads the student *out*, not *in* to, the confines of duplicate testing for all. Finally, standardized testing in subject areas essentially smothers original thought, both because of its single-track mentality and, more fatally, because of the irresistible pressure on teachers to teach to the tests.

Clearly, the political goal of the standards movement is to demonstrate evidence of improvement. And the easiest way to accomplish that objective en masse, deceiving as it may be, is through standardized test scores. We know that focused preparation for a specific test tends to produce higher scores. But we know also that short-term drill, though it may produce a performance, does not produce an educated man or woman. Independent schools in America have been in business for hundreds of years, and we do not survive because we are naïve or timid about our convictions. Once again into the breach!

FOOLING THE PEOPLE

Bulletin 257, April 2001

It was, of course, inevitable that, sooner or later, parents who understand the meaning of education would challenge New York State's current policy on mass testing. The story appeared on page 1 of the April 13 issue of *The New York Times*:

> Scarsdale, N.Y., April 12 – Parents and school officials in this affluent suburb, where test scores are among the highest not only in the state but also in the nation, are planning a coordinated revolt against state standardized tests, saying they have stifled creativity and forced teachers to abandon the very programs that have made the schools excel.
>
> The parents of some 100 eighth graders—a third of the class—have pledged to keep their children home from school when tests are administered in that grade next month. They are doing this with consent, and even subtle advice, from school officials, who administer the tests.

Although the language is somewhat different, the sentiment of Scarsdale parents and school people exactly reflects the independent schools' position of the last five years. Over and over we have said that one-size-fits-all content-based testing destroys curricular autonomy (which is the reason for our being), stifles originality, and demoralizes teachers whose performance is judged by standardized test scores. The saddest aspect of compulsory state testing is that it is essentially a political, not an educational, solution to a social problem. The quickest way to get poor performing schools and students to look better is to raise scores on prepackaged tests. Everyone knows that single-focus preparation produces at least some improvement from virtually any group. But to tell the general public that such training for tests raises educational standards is an abomination.

As the present cycle of "educational reform" winds down, we begin to see cracks in the heretofore unyielding edifice. There is talk of vocational diplomas, of retaining the Regents Competency Tests for special-education students, and of considering the pleas of alternative schools for more flexibility. The one thing we know absolutely after a century of research is that the best and deepest learning never results from rigid teaching and a monolithic curriculum. As we hear at last from the parents of Scarsdale, it really is true that you can't fool all of the people all of the time.

SCHOOL REPORT CARDS

Bulletin 208, May 1996

Advocacy for public report cards on school performance has become the order of the day in educational reform circles. The idea is that wide publication, presumably in the media, of enrollments, staff ratios, racial and ethnic distributions, test scores, drop-out rates, numbers earning diplomas, postsecondary plans, and such will stimulate (or embarrass) all schools toward better performance. The idea is based in its milder form on shame avoidance, that is, that people will work harder to avoid public humiliation. In its sterner form there is the threat of reprisals like job loss and organized attacks. The ancient philosophical question, of course, remains unresolved: which is the stronger motivator, the promise of love or the fear of death?

A strong case can be made that public schools should report to the public, which they do not comprehensively do now. After all, untold billions of taxpayer dollars pay for the colossus that is public education, and, surely, citizens have the right to know to what effect their money is spent. Furthermore, the discipline of required annual or more frequent reports focuses leaders and others on specific goals, and forces debate on the validity of both content and measurement. Finally, public report cards make concealment, if not tampering, more difficult.

But to require such report cards of private schools is an entirely different matter. In the view of many, private schools have the obligation to report on their performance to their patrons, who are not the public but are those who pay tuition for the service. Private schools also have the obligation, many believe, to report to the state, which has the right to know that *all* students are being adequately educated. The biggest difference between public and private, however, is choice. Public-school parents essentially have no choice about where their children attend. Good, bad, or indifferent, the public school continues. At worst, it may be seized by the state, or get even more resources to help it along. Choice, on the other hand, governs the survival of private schools. Children are enrolled or withdrawn at will, based upon the satisfaction of the user.

If private schools were compelled to publish massive profiles, there could be chaos in the marketplace. Schools with bright students, despite mediocre teaching, would look good. Schools with average students, despite great teaching, would look less good. The myriad missions of private schools would be incomprehensible in the welter of the media blitz. To distinguish carefully and thoughtfully between schools that no one *has* to attend would be impossible for most people. The present, relatively civilized competition of private schools would be torn to pieces, and only the enemies of private education would benefit. If public schools want school report cards, that is their business and maybe their salvation. It is not ours.

TAKING THE FIFTH

Bulletin 215, February 1997

It is, apparently, the declared intention of *U.S. News and World Report* to do for private schools what they have done for American colleges and universities. Each year the magazine publishes a guide that ranks our institutions of higher learning in various categories: large and small, teaching, research, and so on. To acquire the data for the rating edition *U.S. News*, amazingly, gets all the colleges and universities to fill in questionnaires. It's probably fair to say that the vast majority of participants hate the exercise, but somehow feel helpless to do otherwise. It is alleged that Stanford University has decided to resist and to sue if misrepresented. Bravo!

The case for the vaunted guide is basically threefold. It entertains the public and makes gobs of money for *U.S. News*. It provides some families a slightly voyeuristic and certainly superficial method of making distinctions between American colleges. It demonstrates that it's still a free country. Other than that, it's an abomination.

Bad as the college exposé is, to try to "unmask" independent schools for the delectation of the reading public is worse. Practically everything our schools stand for is sullied by the process. The unhealthy matching of schools with hopes for prestigious college placement would be further exacerbated. Younger children whose schools had been ranked but who would not understand the arbitrariness of the system would be confused and ashamed, while older students would either strut or slink, as the case may be. Many parents who are already hooked on status would be even more frantically drawn into the race.

But, most important, the point of being private schools, that is, to be what you want to be, to teach how you want to teach, to serve whom you want to serve, would be compromised and even lost in a welter of misleading and shallow "statistics." The real travesty of such commercially driven surveys is that they purport to clarify, when they actually distort. The complexity of private schools—their origins, their purposes, their resources—defies analysis by some glib questionnaire whose sole intent is the excitement of hyped-up competition.

The scattering of Mahatma Gandhi's ashes in the Ganges River last month reminds us of the enormous power of passive resistance. To produce such a survey of private schools as *U.S. News and World Report* proposes requires our cooperation. Without consistent responses to the same questions from every school, no credible report can go forward. If all independent schools simply refused to respond, the project would collapse. To collect and make sense of the bits and pieces of information already in the public realm would be a colossal administrative undertaking with incomplete results at best. At some point the magazine would have to cut its losses. Just as *U.S. News* has the right to publish practically anything it wants, our schools have the right not to testify about themselves. So though we may esteem the First Amendment despite its excesses, this time, for heaven's sake, let's take the Fifth.

OBSESSION

Bulletin 298, May 2005

Newsweek magazine has recently apologized for a horrendous story about interrogation at Guantánamo. It ought to apologize for the May 16 issue on America's "best" high schools. Let's acknowledge that Americans are obsessed with ranking and winning, some of which sadly emanates from the sports world, but not all, by any means. So *Newsweek*'s understanding of Americans' love of contests does not surprise. Other magazines learned long ago that ranking schools and colleges sells. A reporter asked me once why Americans love to read about school winners and losers. I replied, "Why do people go to cockfights? Because they like to go doesn't mean we encourage it." If someone wants to drink too much, do we say, go ahead? From every point of view that originates in even a modest moral sense of what is good for children, ranking schools is an abomination.

It's important to review the absurdities of *Newsweek*'s analysis, if for no other reason than to clear the record. First, the magazine identifies the one hundred best public high schools out of a total of 27,468 or .00364. That's 36/100 of 1%, a fine line by any standard. Second, to justify this singular achievement *Newsweek* tells us that the sole basis for judgment is the number of Advanced Placement tests (and, in a few cases, International Baccalaureates) taken by students in 2004 divided by the number of graduating seniors in a particular school. This calculation produces a ratio which, mirabile dictu, gives us the one hundred best high schools in the United States. Now is it true that schools with the largest number of students taking AP exams proportionate to their size have a larger group of bright students or are they merely pushing APs? And has the AP been chosen by great educators in the sky as the nonpareil of tests that measures best the cerebral excellence and accomplishment of the young? And is performance on any test the best indicator of what it means to be an educated person? As Richard Day, the principal of Exeter in the 1960s, once said to his faculty, "It's not that you teach so brilliantly, it's that you have some of the brightest students in the country." The comment did not go down well.

Thankfully, there is only one independent school mentioned in the article, and that is because it eschews APs and offers interesting alternatives to aspiring students. The point, of course, to be made over and over again is that the best schools are those that draw the most from whatever kind of students they have, so that it can truly be said at the end of the process that these students have met or exceeded their capacities. Independent schools know this, and at bottom this is what we do. We know also that the kind of people we produce is as important as the kind of intellects we hone. Ultimately, it is the quality of the decisions our graduates make in life that will justify our work. If it were only so easy as training for tests.

THE POLITICS
OF EDUCATION

Bulletin 195, February 1995

Once confined to the relative stability of the classical curriculum, American education is now rife with politics. State education commissioners, defending their agendas and enumerating their achievements, resign in frustration as new governors begin their terms. Terrible battles over money between mayors, unions, and education bureaucracy are waged. Social studies curricula, written by panels of "experts," float from one pressure group to another, each claiming unfair treatment or massive distortion. Legislators fling bills into the hopper regulating schools to teach everything but academic subjects (like how to avoid abduction or care for the flag) that families used to teach as a matter of course. Altogether it's a horrible mess.

Historians of oppression tell us that the classical curriculum was just as political as the present morass. The difference, they say, was that there was only one politics, those of the North European white male and his descendants. What appeared to be agreement about the goals of American education was actually the submission of the disenfranchised and powerless. The canon, which stood for so long, is now justly crumbling under the righteous assault of those once left out.

The value of a canon, any canon, is threefold. First, it delivers whatever about it is worthwhile in a coherent, reliable framework.

Second, it gives all its recipients something solid and predictable against which to sharpen their critical faculties or even to rebel. Third, it prevents the chaos of approaches and programs that risks apathy in the young and the unity of society. Multiple canons, of course, have the advantage of offering everybody's version of the truth. The big questions for all educators in the late twentieth century may well be: how many versions can our young people take, and what is the end of uncontained credibility?

Independent schools are less susceptible to political forces than their public sisters, but they are far from immune. The moral and intellectual chaos of the larger society washes over us too. While independent schools are theoretically free to teach any curriculum they want, most offer a kind of revisionist version of the classical canon. The goal of revisionism is rightly to admit a broader truth. But the danger of the present time in the United States is that we are in profound transition. As independent schools traverse the political minefields, the clarity and conviction of their missions are paramount. We are still free within limits to decide who we are and what we stand for. To be timid in an age of rampant politicization is a guarantee of disaster.

DECONSTRUCTING EDUCATION

Bulletin 212, October 1996

To considerable fanfare on October 8, New York Governor George Pataki signed legislation that requires all children over the age of eight to study the mass starvation in Ireland from 1845 to 1850. It should be noted that this act is not merely a suggestion or a guideline, or even a regulation; it is the law of the land. Private schools that fail to comply with the law's provisions may lose their equivalency status, which is the legal basis for their existence. Senator Michael Hoblock of Albany, who sponsored the bill and whose district is 27% Irish American, said: "The intended purpose of this legislation is to raise public awareness of the factual causes of the mass starvation. . . . We must ensure that our children are educated to learn from past wrongs."

The Albany *Times Union* quotes Governor Pataki at the signing ceremony in the capitol as saying, "We will become the first state in the country to require teaching our children the *truth* about the starvation in Ireland from 1845 to 1850." Which is to say, in this remarkable assertion, that the other forty-nine states (where the subject is taught) have falsified, misrepresented, or just plain lied about the Great Hunger in Ireland. The governor's assertion also begs the question: does New York State now have the truth about the Irish potato famine, whereas all others have failed? And will the State Education Department's version of the

Irish potato famine prohibit other interpretations or, at best, make them politically risky?

To the criticism from opponents of the law that "politicians were pandering to the Irish vote and setting a precedent for endless requests from other ethnic groups," Governor Pataki replied that lawmakers, if anything, are more suited to make curriculum decisions because they're directly selected by and accountable to New York's citizens. This is to say that a grab bag of legislators from around New York State should micromanage our children's curriculum, so they can be reelected to office. If it were not a matter of record, these utterances would remind us of some terrible Swiftian fantasy. They still do.

The deconstructionists, of course, may have a field day with the Irish potato bill. Deconstruction asserts that all meaning is subjective, and that the best we can hope for is partial truth. Although all educational choices reflect to some degree the interests of the choosers, the classical curriculum that has dominated most of the twentieth century at least attempted to be objective about quality. Or as John Updike says in another context, it presupposed an "enduring truthfulness or a passionate excellence." If we are now consigned to curriculum by political whim, as each faction inserts its social construct, we had better surrender our last illusions of objective reality. And then as teachers and educators surveying our profession, we can ask each other endlessly, "What *does* it all mean?" Or better yet, we can, indomitable to the last in the great tradition of private education in America, fight on!

CULTURE AND COMMUNITY

INTRODUCTION

Fred Calder has always reminded us that school culture lies at the heart of the matter. As independent schools, we are free to define our cultures through the people we hire, the students we admit, the curricula we choose. These are all areas, of course, that are the ultimate responsibilities of the head of each school. But Fred senses something more: as school leaders we do not actually define but rather interpret and communicate our schools' cultures to every member of the community. He modeled this by interpreting the broader landscape of education and society for us in every gathering and in every issue of the *Bulletin of the New York State Association of Independent Schools*.

Fred's wisdom on the culture, curriculum, and community of our schools is conveyed in this section of *Without Apology*. He prods us toward "courage and clarity" in keeping our missions brief and compelling.[1] After all, no one wants to "work hard for a dull idea."[2] He tackles important topics of the day, such as sustainability and technology, and demonstrates why it has been important to care about them in our schools. A historian himself, he navigates easily through the often contentious debates on curriculum that have swirled around the teaching of history, as well as of foreign languages.

Some of his most prescient pieces reflect the growing consumer culture and its impact on our schools. He understands that "snuffing the fires of outrage and perceived injustice" can be wearying, while giving us the courage to be bolder with outrageous parent demands and to stand firm against mounting pleas for special exceptions.[3] In one of my favorite bulletin essays, which

I reprinted for the Nightingale-Bamford community, he identified the "virtue of failure,"[4] at just the moment when anxiety was keeping many parents from accepting anything less than perfection. Fred is delightfully countercultural.

As a New York City school head, I had the pleasure of hearing Fred's reports from Albany in our regular Guild of Independent Schools of New York City meetings three times a year. Always last on the agenda, Fred would open with the salutation "Friends," before updating us on state news and the issues to pay attention to in our schools. Like his writings contained here, his reports were succinct, humorous, and packed with wisdom. He might take a moment to tell us about the byzantine deliberations of New York government or to advise us about resisting state-mandated testing. He somehow managed to highlight the spirit of collegiality and cooperation within our group, while at the same time reminding us to make up our own minds about any issues facing our schools. He sensed what we might be wrestling with in the privacy of our offices.

I always left those meetings inspired about our noble purpose in education and even more dedicated to doing the right thing for the students, faculty, and families at Nightingale. After hearing Fred speak or reading a bulletin, I knew that I was not alone. Whether writing in the 1980s, 1990s, or just last month, Fred captured the mood of our times and urged us toward our best selves.

DOROTHY A. HUTCHESON
Head, Nightingale-Bamford School

1. See "The Primacy of Mission," p. 94.
2. See "The Primacy of Mission," p. 93.
3. See "The Unreality Principle," p. 112.
4. See "The Virtue of Failure," p. 114.

THE PRIMACY
OF MISSION

Bulletin 232, October 1998

It's often said that independent schools are mission driven, meaning, one supposes, that the energy of the enterprise flows from its
understood purposes. If the success of a school is directly proportionate to the degree of motivation and the depth of conviction
of its teachers and leaders, then the idea of the school must be
compelling. We do not work hard for a dull idea. Or to put it
another way, one of the symptoms of a failing institution is the
dullness or irrelevance of its mission. The question, of course, is
what is the content of missions that inspires human achievement?

Religiously based schools in this respect have always had it easier, especially if they are not too timid about their origins. Their
fundamental purposes are rooted in religious belief, which, when
combined with educational goals, can produce formidable momentum. Such schools range from the narrowly denominational to the
broadly inclusive, but in either case may call upon historic com-
mitments and attitudes that define unmistakably what they stand
for. Demonstrated religious faith moves people, even those who
are nonbelievers. Schools that have it in critical mass enjoy high
levels of motivation. And their missions are clear.

Nonsectarian schools, on the other hand, may be hard pressed
to find a compelling purpose. The consumer society, the break-
down of consensus, and the fear of failure all combine to threaten

a wobbly mission. It's not enough to have simply a college prepara-
tory curriculum with all the trimmings (though it's certainly a
good start) or to "want our students to struggle for the apprehen-
sion of universal human truths." Compelling missions need strong
moral content of which their authors are unafraid: this school
requires an atmosphere of civil discourse; this school is based on
unreserved respect for every person; this school insists upon...; this
school does not tolerate...; and so on.

The point is that our present age requires both courage and
clarity in our schools' missions. Though some people may resist
superficially, most are hungry for something firm that goes beyond
the conventional platitudes. And, mirabile dictu, when the moral
content of a nonsectarian school's mission is clear, forceful, and
always honored in the breach, those who work each day with children are energized and motivated to do their best with whatever
they have.

THE SCHOOL AS FAMILY

Bulletin 114, December 1986

The holidays have a way of forcing relatives to spend time together. Some groan at the prospect. Others rejoice. In either event, we feel anxiety. There is, of course, a huge difference between family and friends. The former we acquire; the latter we choose. Family provokes; friends soothe.

Yet friends can be too easy. One or two may last a lifetime. Most come and go, banished when they begin to resemble relatives. Friends share our triumphs with less skepticism than family. Our disasters they often do not share at all. Relatives have no choice but to live through both.

The tribal community of an independent school is more like family, especially when tenures lengthen. As life courses on, there's no escaping each other. Only the students come and go. Yet, as with family, we have to confront the issues together, and, in that crucible of compulsory relationships, we summon the emotional strength to keep the school thriving.

Let the holidays also celebrate family and tribe. Neither lets us off easily, but out of the dynamic of each comes most of the growth we attain. How fortunate we are to have families, and to be school people too.

THE END OF SIMPLICITY

Bulletin 254, December 2000

For much of America December is the month that celebrates our country's spiritual roots. The paradox for many is that it's hard to reconcile the simplicity of the manger with the massive materialism of the Christmas season. In that sense, the twentieth century has not been kind to the cultivation of spiritual life. Ask any head of school whether it is harder in this age than before to acquaint our youth with religious thought and practice. The answer, of course, goes without saying.

One prominent boarding-school head recently spoke of the profligate spending of resources in the 1990s on new facilities that by traditional standards beggar the imagination. Athletic complexes, art centers, natatoriums, media and library centers, science buildings surround our students with physical elegance and state-of-the-art equipment. What, he asked, is the message of this lavishness to students and faculty? Will we, sooner than we think, view some of these expenditures as misappropriations of precious funds that distort the essence of what a school is supposed to be?

We've come a long way from the ideal of a simple log with a student at one end and Socrates on the other. What is it that now affects eternity, the art teacher or the art center? December reminds us of the virtues of simplicity and their connection with fundamental values in life and in school. The hard question for all who teach is how to bring spiritual meaning to our work with children amid the titanic distractions of our physical world. The Christmas season impels us, at least for a moment, to stop and wonder.

SUSTAINABILITY

Bulletin 237, April 1999

Theologian and environmental philosopher Thomas Berry writes that our establishments (political, religious, educational, and economic) "are failing in their basic purposes for the same reason. They all presume a radical discontinuity between the non-human and the human with all the rights given to the human to exploit the non-human. . . . The university, as now functioning, prepares students for their role in extending human dominion over the natural world, not for intimate presence to the natural world."[1]

Most schools and colleges still pay minimal attention to the great issue of planetary survival. A little recycling here, a little energy conservation there, and a few environmental-studies programs comprise most of the effort. Yet if we believe the warnings of science that the present course of Earth's degradation may very well result someday in there being no schools or students, how do we respond as teachers? What is the role of our educational institutions in moving us toward a sustainable future?

Arguing that schools are obligated to contribute to the health and well-being of society through the dissemination of knowledge and values, one can make the case that schools have the moral responsibility to lead in the global transformation of attitudes that is required. But what would a sustainable school look like? It would emphasize sustainability throughout its curriculum, preparing students to contribute to an environmentally sound society. And the school *itself* would function as a sustainable community—adopting appropriate consumption in food and energy, incorporating, wherever possible, sustainable design and landscaping and enhancing ecological diversity. The difference would be that instead of merely acknowledging these imperatives, a school would actually obey them.

1. Thomas Berry, "The University: Its Response to the Ecological Crisis," address at Harvard University, April 11, 1996. http://www.ecoethics.net/ops/univers.htm.

BEHAVIOR
IS THE MESSAGE

Bulletin 263, November 2001

The recent heads' conference at Mohonk Mountain House focused on all the things Americans love to hate or, more accurately, ignore: the impacts of global warming, the destruction of the biosphere, and the waste of Earth's resources. Professor William Moomaw of the Fletcher School at Tufts and David Orr of Oberlin addressed the challenge of achieving a sustainable future within a democratic society that prizes individual freedom and, by the way, individual entitlement. Environmental literacy, ecological design, and economic and social justice, they said, are in effect the elements of survival on planet Earth. Hard words for the American consumer, but we deny them to our peril.

Although the conference at Mohonk was planned before the events of September 11, its fundamental subject was vulnerability, in this case, of the tiny speck in the universe that we call home. Just as the attacks of 9/11 demonstrated the fragility of our defenses in the modern world, the depredations that we visit on the biosphere, though less visible now, may well produce an apocalypse far greater than the worst that any terrorist could deliver. If September 11 awakens Americans, never an easy task, not only to the threat of its immediate enemies but also to the ongoing destruction of our planet, then indeed those tragic hours will not have been in vain.

The missions of our independent schools ostensibly contain a statement of our deepest convictions and most precious values. They speak of our hopes for children whom we presume to educate for world citizenship. They enumerate the methodologies we intend to use to turn the young into rational thinkers who can distinguish right from wrong and who care about their fellow human beings. Although the language may differ, all school mission statements are fundamentally moral declarations that look toward the improvement of humanity and its survival in a better world.

Clearly, the time has come to include in our missions a moral commitment to teaching our children about what is happening to the Earth, and to modeling what it means to be sustainable communities in our own right. Remote as the day of reckoning may still seem, the trustees and heads of our schools today may well have no greater responsibility to succeeding generations than this. Until American students see these understandings reflected in the programs and management of the schools and colleges they attend, why should they take them seriously? As educators, we know one thing: the young do not miss the messages of their elders.

FROM CIVILITY
TO RESPECT

Bulletin 255, February 2001

At a recent meeting of school heads, William Adams, president of
Colby College, spoke about the place of civility in the life of the
academy. Recalling the late 1960s and early 1970s, Adams said that
with the benefit of hindsight he believes that civility probably had
to be suspended to achieve closure on certain crucial national
issues. Among these were the blatant inequities of race and class,
the hypocrisy of the ruling elite, and, of course, the Vietnam War.
But though we have largely restored civil discourse to the envi-
rons of learning, it has been neither easy nor complete. As for the
rest of society, we live with a hodgepodge of expression that ranges
from unbridled vituperation to unctuous courtesy. All agreed, it
seems, that for the kind of education that schools and colleges offer,
namely the examination of ideas, civil exchange is a sine qua non.

As the discussion continued, heads averred that while manners
and civility are not the same, we begin with the very young by
teaching manners. Manners, after all, are the child's first break with
the total egocentricity of babyhood. It is, therefore, both school
and family that lead the child through the various progressions that
at the end produce the more or less rational young adult. But other
questions interposed. Is it the lesson of the late 1960s that issues
of diversity, for example, require uncivil conduct to reach closure?
Is civil discourse self-limiting when fundamental societal changes
are at stake? How do we direct the young in these matters? Do we

suppress incivility under all circumstances, or do we channel it? Is there a third way?

Perhaps, some heads thought, the problem is with the word civility. In the world we have entered it has the ring of preordainment about it, and maybe a touch of elitism. Respect, on the other hand, is a word most people seem to understand. Everyone knows what it means to *dis*... somebody. Respect is more inclusive and can be stretched to embrace major differences. It's easier somehow to be respectfully blunt than civilly blunt. As we grapple in our schools (which cannot at their peril abandon the Socratic ideal) with the redistribution of power and other fundamental changes in our outlook, we will need the methodology of respectful confrontation. And what we need to teach our students and reflect in our own behavior is a model of discourse that unyieldingly pursues the truth without diminishing another's humanity. To find that delicate combination is a huge challenge, but if we who educate the young do not care about the search, why should anyone else?

TYRANNY OF THE MINORITY

Bulletin 214, December 1996

The United States Constitution could never have been ratified without the addition of the first ten amendments. Too many citizens feared the tyranny of the majority, and today we still cherish the content of those famous addenda. But few of us, not to speak of early Americans, could have imagined how effectively small groups would learn to shake the confidence of the majority in our permissive democracy. Minority forces of every stripe always claim they are fighting for a righteous cause (and some are), but within our institutions in the 1990s much of what passes for righteousness amounts to willful disruption. Sadly, the tyranny of the minority, which has already wreaked havoc in the public sector, has spilled over into our schools, and dealing with it thus far has not been one of our shining moments.

What is happening to an alarming degree is that the heads of our schools are trading in their historic responsibilities as educational leaders, institutional managers, resident futurists, and chief diagnosticians for a new role that may be called the management of opposition. Though part of any head's job is to counter the temporary unhappinesses of healthy change, in this case we are talking about the consequences of organized aggression. To be suddenly preoccupied with strategies and tactics for containment, with hostile or semihostile confrontations, and with limited resources with which to deal with organized protest is a demoralizing, enervating and distracting activity. It has, of course, very little to do with the education of children.

The tyranny of the minority takes many forms:

- Parent groups protesting a disciplinary decision or seeking the removal of a teacher or administrator, often accompanied by a rogue trustee.
- Certain faculty members resisting the orderly evolution of curriculum and administrative structure.
- Parent groups, outside of normal channels, seeking representation on the governing board.
- External groups with some insiders fighting the school's legitimate development of its own property.

In all of these cases, and by any objective standards, the schools in question are functioning well; they are full; sound teaching and learning are going on, and admirable performance standards are being met. Yet these successful schools are being systematically destabilized. What is ironic about all of this is that independent schools are more vulnerable to these assaults precisely because they are free, unregulated, and flexible. Yet those very qualities are the basis for a strong response.

The phenomenon of organized opposition afflicts only a few schools at a time, but all are subject to its power. Like governments, institutions can forestall trouble by anticipating it. Someone in the school should be constantly vigilant. Boards and heads should regularly think about it. Even a standing committee on stabilization, or some such, may not be too radical an idea. Months of chaos and confusion can be avoided by a swift, authoritative response to the first mass mailing. Clear, confident, intelligent statements from board and head can restore equilibrium rapidly. Hesitation, indecision, and apparent ignorance quickly feed the fires. The point is that we do whatever we have to do to protect our mission from the depredations of the spoilers. We owe that to the dedicated people who labor every day to fulfill the purpose of a school and especially to our reason for being, the young.

THE SCHOOL AS VICTIM

Bulletin 205, February 1996

At a recent meeting of division heads, the leader of the session asked, "What are the dominant stories in the faculty rooms of your schools?" The answer was quick and unanimous: "We're besieged by parents who expect us to do everything they want. And if we resist, the administration doesn't back us up." Of course, the dominant stories are not the only stories and may not even reflect the whole truth themselves. But, as we know, what people believe happened is just as important as what actually happened.

Far too many of *our* schools, from teachers in the classroom, administrators in their offices, and trustees in the boardroom—not to mention the public sector—have step-by-step surrendered their authority. Children respond to correction with claims of rights abuse. When asked to perform a simple task that would help the school, some demur and inquire, "What have you done for me lately?" Grades are routinely and vigorously protested with more aggression than anyone over forty could imagine. And, surely, the undeniable reality of grade inflation cannot be explained solely by the brilliance of postmodern students.

Parents feel free to accost teachers and administrators, partly because there is no penalty for such behavior. They come armed with righteous indignation and the dreaded threat of a lawsuit— which is not to say that parents are always wrong, but that there is an acceptable and an unacceptable way to deliver grievances. Only a school that is itself pathologic would fail to respond to a civilly presented insight in aid of a child. In the highly charged atmosphere of contemporary discourse, there is little tolerance for resistance to a declared position. Thus many conversations begin with howitzers blazing to neutralize the "opposition" before it can react.

From a position of conviction and strength, our schools have moved to the defensive. In one sense, we are living out the cliché about people who behave like victims being treated like victims. The dominant stories in the faculty rooms are self-fulfilling. They invite both the bullies and the response the bullies seek. But the dominant stories are delusional, since our schools have never been better, have never delivered such an array of services to the young, and have never contained so much raw talent among teachers and staff. The paradox of unparalleled excellence and the loss of authority is almost incomprehensible.

Independent schools have enormous authority in law and philosophy. They are supposed to use it. Not to use it in the face of provocation is bad for children, bad for teachers and parents, and bad for the school. Everyone knows what constitutes provocation. It is rudeness in any form, bullying, absurd demands, tantrums, and all the rest. Schools may ban families, students, or anyone else from the premises for virtually any reason. If a lawsuit is even hinted at, the antagonist should be handed the business card of the school's attorney and invited to leave. There is no case that can be made for allowing intimidation.

The great progressive conservative, Theodore Roosevelt, was an advocate of the habit of speaking softly and carrying a big stick. As a child, his puny body and various ailments made him feel weak and ineffectual. His dominant story, no doubt, was victimization by stronger boys. Later in life he wrote in his memoirs: "There were all kinds of things of which I was afraid at first, . . . but by acting as if I was not afraid I gradually ceased to be afraid." In our age of unbridled confrontation, our schools, if they will, could start telling an alternative story.

WHY US?

Bulletin 121, September 1987

During the summer a reporter from a county newspaper called. He was writing a story for the Gannett chain on independent schools in the area. Why, he wanted to know, would a family pay lots of extra money for a private education when surrounded by strong public schools? A good question, and for NYSAIS schools, a crucial one.

Putting aside the less attractive reasons that motivate a few, social status, hoped for admission to a prestigious college, or what have you, I tried to articulate an answer that, I thought, would go to the heart of the matter. Fundamentally, I said, under the circumstances you describe, parents want what the Quakers used to call a "guarded" education for their children. They are paying, of course, for smaller classes, more supervision, manageable athletics, and a longer day. But, above all else, they are paying for the probability that a significant number of experienced adults will know their children well and help them cope, through wise teaching and careful guidance, with a precarious world. They are paying, in short, for the hope of an extended family.

If all of that is close to the truth, the challenge for us is immense. But it is made easier by the certain knowledge that at our best we are models of what schools for all children ought to be.

WHAT DO PARENTS WANT?

Bulletin 157, April 1991

A recent nationwide public-opinion poll commissioned by the Independent Education Fund (a creature of the National Association of Independent Schools) discloses that parents believe individual attention and teaching excellence are the most desirable qualities of schools. The purpose of the poll is to learn what it is that does or could make independent schools attractive to families not now connected with them.

Who among us frail human beings ("alone and afraid in a world we never made," to paraphrase A. E. Housman) doesn't want individual attention? Can there ever be enough? And who does not want for herself or her children the most brilliant, absorbing, original teaching since Plato? The question is whether independent schools can even partially fulfill the fantasy of all parents, that is, nonstop loving support that they do not provide and focused, creative teaching that transcends the popular culture. It's a formidable assignment.

The difficulty is that individual attention (read small classes) and teaching excellence are to a great degree mutually exclusive. The economics of private education in the 1990s, with few exceptions, no longer allows both. Generally speaking, individual attention requires low student-teacher ratios. Great teaching requires high salaries and state-of-the-art facilities. If the choice for parents is small classes and mediocre teaching or larger, not huge, classes and excellent teaching, is there really any choice at all?

Happily, the issue of individual attention is not solely related to low ratios. There are many private schools in which the teaching load exceeds eighty students, but in which students feel cared for. Attention to young people is as much attitude and behavior as it is volume of staff. Give us strong teachers who care for young people and are unafraid of hard work, and whom we care for by paying them well and meeting their professional needs. Then not only will our schools survive and flourish but the parents of the NAIS poll and their millions of unsung compatriots will come close to realizing their dream.

THE PAIN
OF SEPARATION

Bulletin 297, April 2005

The question keeps coming up: is it OK to expel, in effect, whole families from our schools for unacceptable behavior? Most heads and boards understand that if a school is just a little careful in its policies and procedures, there is no legal issue whatsoever. This means that independent schools are contract institutions. The school sets the conditions for attendance, parents agree to them, and the contract is sealed. A recent case in the state of Washington once again confirms the deal. Seattle Country Day School denied reenrollment to three siblings based on their mother's harassment of the school. She sued for breach of contract, lost in court, and appealed. The higher court agreed with the trial court that the school "has the right to dismiss any student . . . who is not making satisfactory progress, has engaged in conduct that is detrimental to the school, or whose parent has engaged in conduct that harms the school." Further, the court said that the "head of school has sole discretion to decide on the mother's conduct." So much for legality.

Though contracts need not be explicit or even in writing (remember breach of promise), it's clearly easier to have a simple statement in the enrollment agreement that the school may sever its connection with a family for any reason that it deems is in the school's best interest. Some enrollment agreements contain other provisions about payments, due dates, or whatever the school wishes, but simplicity should be the goal. Contracts of all kinds have a way of adding complexity in the belief that some- one's interest will be better protected, but when endless provisions start stumbling over each other, it may turn out that what we thought would be clear is not clear at all. School policies that appear in a handbook, for example, an enumeration of disciplinary actions including expulsion, may also be considered a contract and have the same force as a signed enrollment agreement. Where schools become vulnerable legally is when they promise certain proce- dures leading to action and then fail to observe them. So schools are best served by simply stating their right to severance and remain- ing noncommittal on procedures. "The less said the better" is a cliché because in this case, among many others, it's true.

Thus while the legal aspects of severance are relatively easy, the cultural, ethical aspects are not. Independent schools as a group are intensely humane institutions. We hate to give up on a child, even on a parent. The essence of education is growing from mistakes, of learning to walk by falling. We are in the business of another chance to get it right. And we are highly inventive in designing alternatives to severance and in developing rationales to avoid it. The legendary headmaster of Deerfield, Frank Boyden, is said to have actually expelled only six students during a sixty-four-year reign. On the other hand, he was a master of rule by guilt, which is much harder to accomplish these days. In the end, however dif- ficult and wrenching it is, the right and sometimes the responsibility to separate certain people from our communities is one of the absolute prerequisites for the success of independent schools. For whatever it is that our missions and cultures insist are their basic tenets may not be ultimately compromised, or there can be no peace and there can be no learning.

THE UNREALITY
PRINCIPLE

Bulletin 221, September 1997

On a stunning summer day when I was feeling that most, if not all, was right with the world, my reverie was blasted by a bumper sticker. It said, "Second place is the first loser." I wondered about what kind of mind could have invented the concept and, second, about the driven pathology of the bumper's owner. Maybe it was the same person. But most of all I thought about how this sticker summarized an attitude that now suffuses much of what happens in our schools and elsewhere. Taken as a whole, aspects of this phenomenon have nearly destroyed the virtues of competitiveness and transformed the headship from first teacher to corporate defender.

So much of what heads deal with in the 1990s relates to snuffing the fires of outrage and perceived injustice. Failure of any description has become a sentence of death. Every time a student is expelled these days, we are told that it will ruin his life, which is, of course, utter rubbish. It may actually save her life. Yet all of education is based on original inadequacy, from learning to walk to the development of every skill we acquire. The whole Socratic method leads the student out from a failure of understanding to some higher plane of enlightenment. The massive insecurity that undergirds our bumper sticker is both astonishing and highly destructive for our young. I can think of no other method than intense education at every level to begin reversing the trend. Otherwise we and our children are indeed cursed.

The runaway distortions of reality, which seem sometimes ubiquitous, reflect the panic of our late-century culture. They compel people in authority to keep restating the truth. Salutatorians are not losers. Silver medalists are not losers. Competitive standing is not life, and on and on. Heads of school, with what little credibility they have left, must constantly resist distortion in all its forms. A wise professor of mine once said, "Tell people anything three times and they'll believe it." We have to keep clarifying experience over and over again in the 1990s. It can be boring. It is certainly exhausting, but it is also essential. For if heads and other leaders do not, in our present manic state, we will reap the whirlwind of unreality.

THE VIRTUE OF FAILURE

Bulletin 228, May 1998[1]

We have . . . to restore the virtue of failure to our lives and espe-cially to our children's lives. Now, clearly, I'm talking about discrete failure, not total failure. I'm talking about the interruptions in the success curve that make growth possible. I'm talking about what I believe to be true, that part of learning to walk is falling down.

But something has happened in our schools and in our colleges, which makes no sense at all and which is ultimately deeply destruc-tive. Failure has become intolerable. If you're flunking a course in college, you have the option of dropping it practically up to the final exam. Anything less than a B is considered a black mark for life. In schools and colleges all punishments for wrongdoing are routinely contested as unfair, insensitive, or tyrannical. And, of course, in the most serious circumstances, when a child is asked to leave a school for behavioral or academic reasons, we are told that such an eventuality will "ruin his life." In truth it will in all likelihood save his life by awakening certain actions that will serve his best inter-ests far more effectively than his present situation.

What is really sad about this new phenomenon, that is, the intol-erance of failure, is that much of it stems from a perversion of modern learning theory. In its most simplistic form, as articulated in New York State's so-called student bill of rights, the mantra has become, "All students can learn," which is about as informative as declaring, "All people can eat." The perversion, of course, comes when the word *anything* is added to "All students can learn," whereas we know that the truth is, "All students can learn something" within the limits of their family, school, and societal environments. The root of this sophistry reaches, unhappily, into a misappropriation of learning theory that proclaims that every brain is trainable under the exactly right conditions, that there is theoretically a perfect educational program, setting, and teacher for every child.

Even if there were a perfect educational program for each child, which is doubtful (there are probably only better or worse), our chances of getting it are about one in a million. The upside of all of this thinking about how children learn is that many schools *have* recognized differences in learning styles among children and, to the best of their ability, have adjusted curriculum and methodology to help more children learn. The downside is that the level of expectation for success, largely driven by political rhetoric, has far outstripped anyone's ability to produce.

Now, obviously, these attitudes are not universal. There are still many parents and even children who take their share of responsibility. But they are pervasive enough that they are seriously debilitating our educational institutions and exhausting those who teach and administer within them. The real danger, of course, is that we are raising a generation to believe not that the pursuit of happiness but that success itself is a right, and that failure of any kind is someone else's fault. And down that road lies pain far greater than any discomfort that may be connected with a failing grade or a three-day suspension or being admitted to Yale and not to Harvard. In my judgment this is a course that we must reverse, if we really do care about the health and future happiness of our children.

1. Excerpt from remarks to parents at Ethical Culture Fieldston School, Bronx, New York, May 6, 1998. Fred Calder served as interim head there for the 1997–98 school year.

SUBJECTS AND CHILDREN

Bulletin 118, May 1987

Not long ago people used to argue, sometimes hotly, about whether it was better to teach the subject or the child. Those who taught subjects saw themselves as serious pedagogues steeped in their discipline, transmitting the culture to the untutored and unformed, civilizing the young. The best of them believed passionately in the supreme importance of their subject. The worst were task-masters who disguised their limitations in the dreary expostulation of their field. Nearly all of them were disdainful of people who taught children.

The child-centered people thought about how children learn, about the mysteries of cognition, and about methods of teaching. They believed that John Dewey had discovered at least some new truths. They were less interested in subject matter than in educability. And they were sure that the central academic issue for children was not what they learned, but that they learned.

Other people wished fervently that the teachers of subjects and the teachers of children could get together. When the Russians seemed to pull ahead in the 1950s, the subject advocates took charge. When the country was rent by inner turmoil in the 1960s and 1970s, the child advocates were dominant. And now in the 1980s, as academic standards decline and parents stop being parents, we have at last no choice but to teach both the subject and the child.

It is sad, in a way, that dire circumstances should compel us to do what we should always have done. But people in education are generally no more prescient than anyone else. No longer can any-one ignore the emotional health of our students. No one can minimize the importance of strong skills and certain knowledge. It is easier, of course, to teach either the subject or the child. Doing both takes strength and time and boundless energy. Teachers earn their summers.

THE DISAPPEARANCE OF CONTENT

Bulletin 175, February 1993

In a sense, content has disappeared from the curriculum of our schools. Not because we have really eliminated it, but because the proportion of content to the available whole is so minuscule, compared to a century ago, that to call it comprehensive is a bad joke at best. Some schools still teach largely what was known or was thought to be important a hundred years ago. Then, such content could claim to be inclusive. Today it is not only old but astonishingly limited.

Many educators believe that subject matter is less important than the uses to which it is put. If the goals of teaching history, for example, are to plumb human behavior, to infer from facts and absent facts, and to develop critical skills, then it doesn't matter much what history we study. Ancient is as good as modern. Chinese is as good as Russian. But if the goal of history courses is to teach students where they come from and who they are, then subject matter is paramount. It had better contain much European colonial and lots of American.

The same is true of literature. If the goals are to study the uses of language, the possibilities of literary form, and the vast range of artistic expression through words, then our choices from the corpus of world literature are virtually limitless, even good choices. But if the goals of studying literature are to peer more deeply into our own culture, sharpen our self-definition, and better understand our destiny, then we had best read the works of our immediate forebears and lots of American writers.

Some curricular issues are, of course, relatively simple. If we want to study advanced mathematics, we had better know elementary and intermediate. If we will need to be fluent in German for our professional or business career, we had better study German quickly! But aside from such practical imperatives where the choice is clear, the eruption of knowledge and information in the postmodern world has complicated our task as educators beyond imagining. And the easiest way to avoid that complexity is not to address it.

Curricular content in most American schools is driven by habit and conformity. In most schools changes are marginal, cautious, and teacher-centered. We will not break the logjam, unless we begin seriously to examine our curricular *goals* far beyond the banalities of the typical school catalogue. Why are we teaching history? Why science, literature, and mathematics? What do we hope our students will have when they complete our programs? Most schools do not rigorously consider these questions in ways that lead to major reevaluation, that challenge the shibboleths of standardized testing, and that begin to discover the possibilities of digital technology.

As the content of our curriculum grows smaller relative to the whole and more antiquated relative to the explosion of knowledge, we run the risk of obsolescence. The turn of a century is as good a time as any to start asking the big questions again.

CONCEPTS WITHOUT CONTENT

Bulletin 204, December 1995

In the face of abysmal ignorance, we hear the refrain: "Our children should at least know the main concepts in American history." Is that really all they should know? Is it even possible to *know* just the main concepts?

When Secretary of Education Richard Riley announced the results of the National Assessment of Educational Progress in American history on November 1, those who care blanched. Among other things, a majority of the 22,500 test takers had no idea of either the intent of the Monroe Doctrine or the major goal of American foreign policy after World War II. Just 43% of twelfth graders were able to achieve the "basic level," while only 11% were considered "proficient," and 1–2% "advanced." By any standard, it's a frightening profile.

When I taught twentieth-century American history to seniors in the 1960s, we used a rugged college text called *The Growth of the American Republic* by Samuel Eliot Morison and Henry Steele Commager. Admittedly, by modern rules the book was sexist and classist, but it was dense with information, opinion, and interpretation. Morison and Commager, for example, took the view that the New Deal was essentially a conservative movement, since it sought through built-in stabilizers to preserve the capitalist system. Roosevelt, they said, may some day go down as the greatest American conservative since Hamilton.

Can we even consider suggesting such a concept today to the twelfth graders at the basic level and below? When I think of what my students had to know about the New Deal in order to interpret it, the idea of teaching concepts without content seems absurd. To even hint that abstractions can be taught in an intellectual vacuum is ridiculous. We shall know that the end is near when the first high-school course called "The Concepts of American History" is offered.

As people in education and citizens generally despair about the loss of competence in basic subjects, can we agree on four principles for the New Year in at least one discipline?

1. If there's any chance of getting *unum* out of *pluribus* in the twenty-first century, our children must learn lots of American history.
2. The canon must be modified toward inclusiveness, but not abandoned.
3. At a minimum, all students must know the major benchmarks of our history and their attendant facts.
4. Only out of such acquaintance with the events of history will come the conceptual grasp toward which the whole enterprise of education aspires.

AMERICAN MUTES

Bulletin 286, March 2004

In speaking of many things at the annual National Association of Independent Schools conference in Montreal, Carlos Fuentes and Susan Sontag bemoaned the failure of Americans to teach and become fluent in foreign languages. Their complaint was part of a general concern that in its present iteration our country is communicating with the rest of the world not through the subtle understandings of language but through raw power. Be that as it may, Fuentes and Sontag are not the first to condemn our pathetic attempt as a nation to be at least bilingual. It's easy and natural to point the finger at the education profession. Heaven knows, our children "take" foreign language by the millions. So why are we still mutes except in English? Luckily for us, it's not simply that foreign language teachers do a hard job badly, though some may. It's a lot more complicated than that.

This writer is a good example of the foreign language debacle. In the course of my lingual career, I studied (in a manner of speaking) three foreign languages plus Latin. At the end I had the temerity to teach first year Russian to seniors, though I could only read it haltingly and more or less pronounce it. In terms of fluency, I might as well have been teaching ancient Greek. As for my French and German, they were long gone. Now granted, in those ancient times, even contemporary languages were taught primarily to read, not speak, in many American schools, which is better perhaps than no exposure at all. Yet in recent decades, with far more emphasis on the oral and aural, the results are still pretty dismal.

Everyone knows, of course, that the best way to learn language is by necessity. Little children learn language to get what they want and need. Dutch and Norwegian boys and girls learn English in large numbers for essentially the same reasons. But American children know instinctively that if you are at the top whoever needs you will speak your language, not theirs. And then to lock it all up, English has become the lingua franca of the world. So the motivation for learning new sounds and words and structures of a second or third language, which for most people is very hard work, is limited indeed. The truth is that among all our teachers, even the best, the most Sisyphean job by far is performed by those who try to teach young Americans foreign language.

Yet, knowing these things to be true, our schools go on doing over and over that which does not work, the classic definition of neurosis. The political will, as it were, to make foreign language a necessity fails. Virtually no school is willing to choose *one* second language and force it to suffuse the institution from bottom to top: have it required at mealtimes, obtain a large proportion of faculty fluency, and so on. No school is willing to teach at least one mainstream course, for example, science or history, in a second language. Few schools, if any, mandate a semester of language immersion abroad. If children, as they do in other cultures, perceived foreign language as a necessity, they would learn.

In some ways, the worst thing educators can do is to proclaim the importance of a subject area, spend hundreds of millions on personnel, space, and equipment (remember language labs), and never deal with the underlying connections that would make it effective. Of all the hypocrisies in precollegiate education, this may well be the worst. In most human undertakings, if it is not worth the effort, we don't do it. Why then do we persist in this expensive fiction? We seem to know we should, but we can't.

THE TECHNOLOGY REVOLUTION IN LEARNING

Bulletin 184, December 1993[1]

Many of you, I am sure, are more familiar than I with the wonders of digital technology, which brings text, sound, and visuals together in one computerized format.

What is important about all of this in my view is that digital technology is on the verge of transforming teaching and learning, and that it is imperative both for its own sake and for the healthy survival of our private schools that we be in the forefront of these seminal changes. The skilled teacher of the future, even the immediate future, no longer cleverly imparts and explicates and coaxes (although there will always be a place for performance teaching). Rather he designs a learning experience through the sight, sound, and text of digital technology, in which several students relate to each other and to the medium in a dynamic collaboration. Grounded in her knowledge of her field, the teacher as organizer becomes the coach as strategist.

But the difference this time is not cosmetic. This time, I believe, we have taken a millennial step beyond which students will learn much more much faster. The coming of interactive learning will also be the catalyst for the long overdue, fundamental revision of the American curriculum. Digital technology gives us the chance to break up the old Gutenberg system of studying and reproducing, and adapts easily to the specialization of knowledge within great contexts that surely will be the wave of the future.

Although some of our schools are already in the vanguard, not enough are. The private-school culture tends to idealize the past, when students knew right from wrong and accepted their elders' disapproval, when great charismatics bestrode our campuses, when students and teachers and parents all knew their places, and when a classical education was meet and right for all young people of the better classes. Obviously, we must never surrender the fundamental values that undergird our independence, but in this case we must not wait to see what happens. The technology revolution in learning probably presents the greatest opportunity for educational leadership in several centuries, and only at our peril do we leave its undertaking to others.

1. Excerpt from remarks to Independent Schools Chairmen's Association.

LEADERSHIP

INTRODUCTION

W̶hat an honor it has been to work so closely with Fred Calder through my tenure as a New York State Association of Independent Schools trustee. That in itself has been a seminar on leadership, as, through our conversations and his advice and example, Fred has taught me much about perspective, balance, clear communication, humor, and thoughtful responses rather than reactive ones. I have taken that advice and applied his example to numerous situations, both professional and personal, and always with good results. How enjoyable and worthwhile it was to read through Fred's writings on leadership—and trustees, administrators, and, of course, school heads—as I prepared to write this introduction. Doing so made me say, "Yes!" and "Aha!" and "Exactly!" just as I did when I read his bulletin texts for the first time.

For me, Fred's writings and his speeches have been a beacon of clarity and direction in a sea of confusion and contradiction about leadership. I know I am not alone. Common sense, common courtesy, and courage are the bedrock of Fred's view of leadership. Above all, he keeps our focus on "the people for whom the community is supposedly organized . . . students."[1]

Consider some of these gems from the man I consider to be the independent-school philosopher-king:

On leadership:

> Independent schools are and should be accountable to those who
> patronize them, but they have the responsibility also to challenge
> their constituents with visions of our children's future.[2]

The challenge for today's head is to orchestrate strategic thinking, to lead the team in this method of thought, and to supply the discipline that makes sure it happens.[3]

The legitimacy of the head's authority has been diluted. Second guessing, endless consultation, and wishy-washy compromise are the order of the day.[4]

Despite its current disfavor, obviously, no must still be said, or we risk anarchy.[5]

When the next abomination crosses your desk, do not panic, but instruct your advisors to find a way out for your school.[6]

The school and its people will do everything humanly possible to protect the children in their care, but if there is to be a functioning, dynamic institution, all must accept a measure of risk.[7]

On trusteeship:

In the postmodern independent school there simply is no more important relationship than that of the head and board head.[8]

Being a trustee . . . these days takes stamina, where once it didn't take much. The stakes are higher. Exposure is greater. Time is shorter, and demands are bigger. The least we can do for these unpaid volunteers is to husband their time and energy, keep them from boredom, and make their work important.[9]

On hiring and evaluation:

We need two qualities for a successful independent-school teacher or administrator. One is high intelligence, and the other is emotional stability.[10]

If the key leaders in a school (in this case, chairman, board, and head) are competent and confident, informal evaluation of performance is by far the most effective and efficient way to proceed.[11]

The head should be evaluated by his employers, not his employees. He is not an elected official.[12]

And, finally, on the role and importance of independent schools:

> In the end, as we ponder the exigencies of world leadership, all
> we have is education, and all we have as independent schools is
> our small but utterly vital part of it.[13]

It has been a privilege for me to have the opportunity to praise
and honor a mentor and friend. All of us involved with independent schools in New York State are so very fortunate to have had
Fred Calder as executive director of NYSAIS for twenty years. We
are luckier still that his wisdom and inspiration remain with us in
his writings.

DREW CASERTANO
Head, Millbrook School

1. Frederick C. Calder, "The Price of Accountability," see p. 132 of this volume.
2. "The Limits of Accountability," p. 135.
3. "Three Perspectives on Strategic Planning," p. 154.
4. "The Perils of Responsibility," p. 162.
5. "Getting to No," p. 136.
6. "Unhelpful Advice," p. 138.
7. "States of Emergency," p. 150.
8. "Head to Head," p. 170.
9. "Respecting Trustees," p. 168.
10. "The Hiring Dilemma," p. 148.
11. "Evaluating Boards and Heads," p. 173.
12. "Evaluating the CEO," p. 175.
13. "Teaching from the Top," p. 144.

THE PRICE OF ACCOUNTABILITY

Bulletin 122, October 1987

There was a time not long ago when the standard for leadership in our schools was limited accountability. All leaders were expected to display attitudes that were in decent conformity to the pretensions of the community. But they were also permitted, if not expected, to make independent judgments on certain issues and at certain times based upon a higher authority that derived from the community's respect for their training, their experience, and their stature.

We have now fully entered a period of total accountability, whereby virtually no educational leader can disregard the wishes of his constituencies except at his peril. The apologists call it participatory democracy; the critics call it mob rule. In either case, to survive requires the suspension of independent judgment and the application of consummate political skills to forge consensus. In places where consensus is impossible, the result is stalemate and the regular removal of leaders to satisfy the community's frustration.

Everyone knows that without accountability, humaneness and appropriateness are diminished, if not eliminated. But when accountability is distorted into a kind of mindless servitude, this time of the leader by the led, then we do finally a profound disservice to the people for whom the community is supposedly organized, in our case, students. The hope is that the present cycle will be short-lived, and that bitter experience will lead again to the essential balance between accountability and judgment. If not, we shall continue down the road to stagnation in our schools until sanity is restored to educational leadership.

THE LIMITS OF ACCOUNTABILITY

Bulletin 155, February 1991

Virtually everyone seems to have read, or read about, John Chubb's and Terry Moe's *Politics, Markets and America's Schools.* Private-school people are thrilled at last to have an "objective" study, from the Brookings Institution no less, that proclaims their superiority. Public-school people are less thrilled, if not to say enraged.

The Chubb-Moe thesis is that private schools as a group are better than public schools because they are controlled by the market, whereas public schools are controlled by democratic politics. Private schools must, therefore, perform since they are directly accountable to their constituencies, who if unhappy will depart, leaving us sitting in our buildings without students. Accountability in public schools, on the other hand, is so diffuse—to elected boards of education, to the state and federal bureaucracies, to courts, legislatures, and governors—that no one feels the fire at his feet. Thus public-school performance generally suffers by comparison.

As appealing as the Chubb-Moe findings may be at one level, they may be less so at another. For while our paying customers, that is, parents, demand and get pretty high performance out of us, the truth is that most parents are short-term thinkers about education and want a reliable, tested product that will get their son or daughter into life's next slot. What keeps parents happy is not

N
Y
S
A
I
S

innovation but a familiar educational menu that is expertly cooked and elegantly served.

So the case can be made that the chances for real, not cosmetic, change in the curriculum we offer the young are more likely to come in a system that does not require immediate accountability to short-term consumer interests. Whereas private education allows fewer abuses, it may also allow less flexibility. While we constantly hail our independence, defend it, advertise it, and equate it with freedom of action, the fact is that most independent schools serve the narrow interests of their fee payers, and in one sense don't have much freedom at all.

Clearly, there's nothing wrong with doing something well that people want. But the challenge for some independent schools is getting their constituencies to want something else. Independent schools are and should be accountable to those who patronize them, but they have the responsibility also to challenge their constituents with visions of our children's future.

GETTING TO NO

Bulletin 241, September 1999

In a well-known book called *Getting to Yes*, Roger Fisher explains the techniques of successful negotiating. Oddly, the problem in our schools these days is not getting to *yes*, it's getting to *no*. In the final blooming of the late–1960s revolution, all requests and behaviors are expected to be affirmed. No and its assorted variations are unacceptable responses that bring charges of unfairness and tyranny. The Moses figure (whom some of our school heads once resembled and even looked like) is no longer understood, much less revered.

A few historians can still recall a time when children, especially adolescents, actually wanted adults to say no. They would never admit it, of course, but a resounding no would make them feel safe and reintroduce rationality into the world. Today's questions from both students and parents often test rationality and can even leave us speechless. Because my son gets nervous in testing situations, can't he have a private setting with unlimited time? Doesn't ADA require the school to do this? If my child needs to ride everyday to prepare for horse shows, can't she be excused from all physical education requirements? What right does the school have to interfere with drinking parties on weekends? How can you punish my daughter for copying a paper that I obtained for her? And on they go toward the millennium.

Despite its current disfavor, obviously, no must still be said, or we risk anarchy. The point is how do our school heads and their besieged administrators say no without losing their tempers (composure?) and alienating their "clients"? Those in the how-to business have some good suggestions:

1. Never take it personally. The anger and anxiety you hear spring from insecurity and fear of failure.

2. Don't argue. Point for point rebuttals in emotional contexts do not change minds, but solidify frustration.

3. Keep raising the level of discourse from "what I want" to the needs of the community and what the school stands for.

4. If there's ever the slightest opening in the conversation, use humor. This can take nerve and skill, but can work wonders.

5. Don't make statements. Ask questions. For example, if we granted your request, could we deny the same thing to everyone else? If we accommodated every child with test anxiety, how could we afford the space and personnel? How do we balance what you want with the school's belief in equity? Do you think the school should be unconcerned if its students are breaking the law? Is this a message you really want your child to hear?

Questions demand thought and require context. They are not of themselves argumentative. If sincerely posed and thoughtfully phrased, they can disperse anger and even inspire understanding. Think of their use as an extension of the Socratic method that still, we hope, undergirds the academy.

It's a difficult time for those in authority, especially in schools where humaneness is a principle and everyone wants to please. But we know also that limits are sacred, and we know who is ultimately responsible for their imposition. As a famous watercolorist and bricklayer once said, "Never give up."

UNHELPFUL ADVICE

Bulletin 116, March 1987

As the world of schools and the world at large grow more complicated, administrators turn to specialists for advice. Lawyers, accountants,
environmentalists, state and local regulators, and other "experts" tell
us what we can and cannot do in the management of our schools.
Much of the advice we get is sound and useful. But much is also
alarmist and overdramatic. There are too many advisors these days
who are not satisfied unless they frighten their clients.

A wise person once said, "We must always dominate our professional help." This means we do not hire lawyers to tell us what
we cannot do but to tell us how to do what is needed and morally
right. To be sure, federal, state, and local legislation has proliferated
in recent years despite the promise of less government. Issues of
equity, employment security, distribution of benefits, medical rights,
and others bombard our schools, where education was once the
main concern. Under the weight of it all, there is a tendency to
cave in and dully conform.

Independent-school people natively resist mass thinking. The
same holds true for mass regulations and mass solutions. Our very
existence as schools is a statement of our belief in unique responses
to the human condition. So when the next abomination crosses your
desk, do not panic, but instruct your advisors to find a way out for
your school. Surprisingly often, they can help, and what appeared
monstrous becomes manageable. Above all begin with the assumption that things are usually not as they appear, and call NYSAIS.

LESS SAID THE BETTER

Bulletin 196, March 1995

The story goes that one of Washington's most charming hostesses
in the 1920s was determined to get President Coolidge to say three
consecutive words or more. One evening at a White House dinner she sat next to Coolidge. After repeated attempts at conversation,
which produced only monosyllabic responses, she said in desper-
ation, "Mr. President, you've got to help me. I've bet several of my
friends that I can get you to say three words or more." Coolidge
turned, fixed her with a stare, and said, "You lose."

Needless to say, such taciturnity is in short supply today. People in education, of course, tend to talk a lot. They believe in
explanation and explication. They think talk heals, prevents vio-
lence, and, above all, reaches children. Education is the preeminent
talking business. Talk is, after all, the major vehicle of humaneness
and, with writing, the primary transmitter of rationality, or what's
left of it. Can it be that school people should start talking less? In
certain respects, the answer appears to be yes.

Schools, in their laudable desire to be open and honest, are
prone to overexplaining. Many admissions offices, for example, feel
obligated to tell parents in detail why they cannot accept a child.
Some even try to ease the blow by suggesting after an elaborate
explanation that the application should be withdrawn. Most schools
are inclined toward long expositions when a student must be suspended or expelled. The need to explain is especially felt when
schools ask an employee to leave. Yet there is no requirement in

law or elsewhere to explain anything to anyone. The problem is that schools generally are institutions of good faith. The tragedy is that in the 1990s good faith is seldom rewarded.

Clearly, independent schools and those who speak for them may be as voluble as they wish. It's still a free country. But administrators should understand that the spirit of *Miranda* applies to them too. Anything they say or write may be used against them. The strongest lawsuits against schools may draw on innocent utterances cleverly converted into contraventions of public policy. In an age when the denial of gratification is by definition unfair, the purest of motives becomes the exemplar of perfidy. It's a sad fact that schools can save themselves untold misery and much money by simply refusing to talk. Considering that he left office only seven months before the Great Depression began in 1929, Calvin Coolidge has come out relatively unscathed. And why not? It's hard to attack someone who doesn't speak.

THE HAZARDS OF TALK

Bulletin 251, September 2000

It's probably never wise to generalize about groups. But if anything can be said with a high degree of accuracy about independent-school people, it is that we talk too much. First, we tend to be a verbal lot; it goes with the vocation. Second, we love to explain *everything* to children, to parents, to each other, and to the world. Third, we are a humane bunch, believing that love and respect for other human beings require elucidation, in great detail if possible.

While much can be said (no pun intended) for our garrulity, in matters of admission and employment, excessive talk can be costly. One of the great independent-school attorneys once said, "Never explain bad news; just give it." He was referring not to institutional breakdowns or the external world, but to the moments when children are denied admission or employees are asked not to return. Being the nice folks that we are, we may find the attorney's warning harsh. In fact, it's not, for it actually avoids much more pain than it causes.

It must be said up front that there is no legal requirement whatsoever for a school to explain why it has rejected an applicant for admission. It is enough to say simply, over and over again if necessary, that the volume of applications compelled the school to disappoint many good people. Parents, of course, want to know exactly why their child failed to get in. And we want to be fair and kind. But the more detail we try to provide, much of it gobbledygook, the less defensible our decision. For each detail may be challenged. Instead of delivering a clear, though disappointing, message, we end up defending a crumbling wall, with lots of distress for all concerned.

Similarly, New York is an "employ at will" state. There is no obligation to explain why someone must leave the institution. Once again, we are vocationally vulnerable. We want to be helpful; we want everyone to understand. But every detail we present is challengeable and could end up in a lawsuit. It is enough to say merely that things have not worked out, or that we have lost confidence in your work. Though our teachers' admonitions to "be more specific" ring in our ears as we sit stony faced, specificity in this case is the enemy, and by eschewing it everyone is spared pain.

So often have we heard in other contexts that the devil is in the details, and, indeed, in these situations it is. If ever in our loquacious work there are times when we should button our lips, these are they. Believe it or not, it's a kindness to all.

TEACHING
FROM THE TOP

Bulletin 278, May 2003

Most of us know intellectually that the United States has arrived at a position of world hegemony probably unparalleled in history. Yet few have internalized its meaning for the generations of young people that stretch before us. Ramsey Clarke, Lyndon Johnson's attorney general, thinks that the U.S. is engaged in acts of militarism that mimic the worst days of Rome. The Bush administration believes that the extension of military might is saving America and the world. The spectrum of thought and speculation between these extremes is immense. But for those who educate the young, it must somehow be navigated within a system of values that preserves life and sustains the Earth. At this historic moment, independent schools in particular should be paying close attention.

In a sense, Americans never asked to sit astride the world (someone spoke recently about how nice it would be to live in Norway, where one may think almost solely of things Norwegian), but there is no alternative in this time and place. Independent schools educate about 1% of all precollegiate American students, and, whether we like it or not, we are preparing them literally for world leadership. This is so partly because of the quality of our work above all other groups of schools, and partly because of the power of our constituencies in American society. A much higher percentage of independent-school graduates finish college and earn advanced degrees than the norm. Call it elitist or what you may, but a much higher percentage of independent-school families function at the most sophisticated socioeconomic levels than the norm. Their influence on politics, public policy, and foreign affairs far exceeds any group of comparable size. And, sadly for the majority of young Americans, as government schools continue to decline, the ranks of independent schools will grow and their impact increase.

One hundred fifty years ago the "public" schools of Great Britain prepared their students to rule the Empire. Far from bearing the white man's burden, independent-school students in the twenty-first century look out on a world, though dominated by America, in vast upheaval. What are the personal values, the analytic skills, the habits of objective thinking about the role of America that these young people will bring into adult life? How will they be prepared to preserve the best of the American experiment and contribute to the peaceful evolution of the rest of the world toward free, self-sustaining societies? The challenge, as always, is to reduce the abstraction to concrete curricular steps across the disciplines. No longer can we afford the nineteenth-century organization of knowledge that still largely predominates. In the end, as we ponder the exigencies of world leadership, all we have is education, and all we have as independent schools is our small but utterly vital part of it.

TRUTH AND THE ART OF HIRING

Bulletin 265, February 2002

The lawsuit epidemic has desecrated lots of human transactions, but none perhaps more than hiring. There was a time when employers sat down and wrote candid appraisals of a person's performance, knowing that the reader expected at least a faint sign of imperfection and that confidentiality would be preserved. Today anyone who dares to write a letter uses code, for example, any characteristic not screamingly superlative is probably bad, or qualities called for but not mentioned are assumed to be lacking. At the ridiculous end of the spectrum are admonitions by attorneys to school heads to provide absolutely no further information than dates of employment and grade levels and subjects taught. This is called the "name, rank, and serial number" rule. It is, of course, an abomination.

Since the written or emailed word is either fatuous or simply not to be believed without tortuous interpretation, what is to be done? There is, alas, nothing left but that ancient piece of nineteenth-century technology, the telephone. And through it there is still, thank heaven, the opportunity to engage in plain speaking with a colleague on *any* subject, but certainly on the subject of a candidate's qualifications. Yet, astonishingly, complaints are made each year by heads of school that a colleague has hired one of their people without making a call. It's difficult to imagine that such an omission is merely an oversight, when hiring decisions are among the most critical a leader makes. But what is even more disconcerting is the possibility that lawsuit intimidation has reached the stage where even a phone call is considered too risky. Let it not be so.

Aside from the ban on truthfulness in our new century, several guidelines still apply to hiring, despite occasional breaches. One is that no school should ever discuss employment with a person already under contract for the period of time in question. Nor should a candidate be interviewed for an immediate job without first notifying his present employer. Candidates should be free, on the other hand, to explore future opportunities in confidence, if they are not under contract for the period of time under consideration. It is primarily the candidate's responsibility to keep her employer informed of job searches, but in the absence of that it is the potential new employer who must insist on such contact. The point of these guidelines, obviously, is to extend common courtesy to all concerned, so that no employer can be accused of piracy and no candidate of failing to meet his moral and legal obligations.

Sadly, in the wider world of education, not to speak of elsewhere, a kind of open season has become the norm in matters of employment practices. But in the independent-school world, for the most part, the remnant lives, and the concept of mutual respect still prevails. When our schools cease to be seekers of truth and respecters of persons, even in this narrow realm, there will be little to distinguish us from anyone else.

THE HIRING DILEMMA

Bulletin 306, March 2006

After a lifetime of hiring and occasionally firing, I confess to an absence of certainty on the subject of a surefire method of success. But I've learned enough to make a few observations that have mostly stood the test of time. Three caveats: first, my theory of good hiring applies primarily to independent schools and more broadly, in some cases, to the nonprofit world. Second, it assumes that the employer has a free hand to define the candidate pool and recruitment technique. Or, conversely, it assumes that the employer is not restricted by seniority rules, union or otherwise, or by pressures from various power centers that may compel "friendly" appointments. And third, given the current popularity of Malcolm Gladwell's recent book, *Blink*, I must at least acknowledge Gladwell's view that a first impression, or blink, may be more accurate than an exhaustive study of the same subject.

What got me thinking again about the matter of hiring was a public radio program in which an attorney/jobs counselor was interviewed for his take on best ways to find employment. Among his many pertinent observations, he said that job hopping is no longer an automatic negative on a résumé, and that, in fact, it is both common and expected. He seemed to suggest that the culture now admires impatience for a better and better situation and frowns on the dull, old, bourgeois virtue of sticking it out. He seemed to be saying in much stronger terms than I would that the bourgeoisie have reached a compromise with the bohemians on employment, as David Brooks declares they have on a number of issues in his book *Bobos in Paradise*. Reluctantly, I agree that there's been some shift in attitude but not by any means seismic.

At some point in my career (a word that is apparently losing its meaning), I developed a theory for successful hiring based on a good deal of experience. I had learned two things, one obvious, one less so. First, the best, virtually foolproof component for making a hiring decision is the *oral* recommendation of a person you know well, deeply respect as a professional, and trust. All else being equal, you can't lose. Second, never hire anyone solely or largely on the basis of charisma.

So what else is there? In the simplest terms, we need two qualities for a successful independent-school teacher or administrator. One is high intelligence, and the other is emotional stability. With an appropriate educational background and acceptable demeanor, chances are excellent that, if you get both qualities, you win. The question is: how do you measure each? The first is relatively easy. If you as the employer deserve to be in your job, you ought to be able to make a face-to-face assessment. Otherwise, and many fail to do this, take a close look at the person's transcript, his or her grades in a challenging program. As for emotional stability, my conclusion was and still is that longevity in a job says a lot about a person's ability to withstand the imperfections of any human organization. In other words, what requires emotional stability is managing the negatives, not enjoying the positives, of one's job. And managing negatives means overwhelmingly not adjusting to the physical environment of the workplace, but dealing day in and day out with the consequences of human behavior and how well you handle them. The system may not be perfect, but in the absence of certainty, it goes a long way toward satisfaction.

STATES OF EMERGENCY

Bulletin 276, March 2003

As our country begins to adopt a siege mentality, so sadly must our independent schools. The challenge in the midst of yellow and orange alerts, warnings of suicide bombers, and apocalyptic visions of radioactive and biologic agents is to be thrivers, not survivors. To survive is to reduce exposure to the minimum. It is to seal off, hide away, and stay put. To thrive is to acknowledge danger, take reasonable precautions, and accept risk. Thrivers lean heavily toward living fully; survivors are content to live at all.

Bombarded as they are by dire alarms, the parents of our students seek reassurance that our schools are safe havens for their children. Thus one more heavy social burden has been visited on our schools. The fundamental issue, of course, is separation. In the event of catastrophe, how do parents know their children are safe? What are the methods of communication? How can the family be reunited? All of these are legitimate fears in the context of disaster. But the beginning of a constructive response is for everyone to understand that there is no fail-safe solution, that good people in our schools will do their utmost for children in any situation, and that when independent schools stop thriving, and start merely surviving, then their reason for being will be gone.

Virtually all schools have had at least the rudiments of emergency or crisis plans in place for years. They include methods of egress, collection points, safe rooms, evacuation routes, location of equipment, and, more recently, storage of food and water. (How quickly we forget the 1950s and 1960s, when government actually supplied our schools with hard tack and drums of water in the event of nuclear attack, when children were trained to crawl under desks.) It's important for schools to publish a summary of basic emergency preparations for all to see, but also to speak frankly about the limits of precaution beyond which there can be no school, only a fortress.

In a recent letter to parents, one NYSAIS head outlined in some detail the school's ample crisis plan, an impressive list of preparations. But toward the end he wrote:

> This is what we do not have in place, nor are we making plans to have them in place:
>
> • We have no duct tape and plastic to seal windows and doors.
>
> • We have no gas masks.
>
> • We have no specialty medicines or other sera for control of biologic or nuclear outbreak, other than regular medical supplies provided by the Nurse's Office.

The message for everyone in the community is that the school and its people will do everything humanly possible to protect the children in their care, but if there is to be a functioning, dynamic institution, all must accept a measure of risk. Whatever the circumstances of our lives, at this moment in history we must be communities of thrivers and builders and learners. There is no other course.

AS WE ARE
OR SHOULD BE

Bulletin 178, May 1993

The revolution in management, though still in its infancy, may yet transform the American corporation from hierarchical structure to learning organization. Both the theoreticians and the practitioners are talking about shared vision, broad empowerment, flatter structures, and "rearchitecturing." Microsoft gloats. IBM shudders.

It's a mistake, of course, to compare nonprofit, independent schools to commercial corporations. School cultures are quite different, though not entirely so. A few private schools are still autocracies. Some are organized hierarchically but not despotically. Many display a kind of modified team management in which the head operates as first among equals, and fellow administrators enjoy major responsibility. In most private schools, faculty members are allowed far more autonomy and originality than "middle managers" in the business world. Though not immune to the malady, schools generally eschew bureaucracy.

The question is whether the churning forces of the information age will require the same radical changes in school structures that corporate thinkers believe must come to commerce and industry. Is it time to stop rewarding specialization and start rewarding multifunctional roles for teachers? Should administrators become team leaders? Should speed and flexibility take precedence over deliberation and tradition? Should schools begin dispersing into the community? Is the classroom, as we know it, approaching obsolescence?

It would be refreshing and truly educating for us all, if at least one independent school would radically reorganize its structure. From mission to strategy to systems to practice, all would be recast. Decision-making would be responsive, never protective. All adults would feel and be responsible. If it didn't work, chances are the damage would be slight, since only the brightest and the most committed would accept such a challenge. But we know that in real life the inertia and risk are simply too huge for fantasies of this scope. Yet summer in our profession is still the time to think big thoughts about how we do things in schools, about whom we are actually serving, and about the fate of young people in America.

Enjoy.

THREE PERSPECTIVES ON STRATEGIC PLANNING

Bulletin 185, February 1994¹

First, it is all the rage in the corporate world these days to repeat the refrain, "It's the customer, stupid!" The theory goes that great companies like GM or IBM were destroyed or nearly destroyed because the power elite decided (arrogantly) what was good for the customer, instead of discovering (humbly) what the customer wanted. I'm not debating the validity of this viewpoint. It may be 100% true for much or all of corporate America. What I do say is, "Beware of transferring such a concept wholesale to private education!"

Clearly, our schools have to perform in ways that please our constituents and have to offer programs and get the results they want. That may be the primary reason we are as successful as we are. But, unlike the corporate world, our schools have the responsibility of transmitting the learning and skills of our culture, which, no matter how it is packaged, will not always be sweet and smooth and succulent. One of our responsibilities is to confront, not to soothe, young people with hard choices, alternative thinking, and difficult problems. Although they will surely have their rewards, these experiences are not always fun.

Across the spectrum from ultraprogressive to conservative our schools have to be in some measure repositories of the counterculture. Whether it's the school that refuses to give up a dress code or requires meeting for worship, community service, Latin, public speaking, sports, or whatever, each of our institutions has a responsibility not to cave in before the temporary dissatisfaction of the young, especially in an age when so many parents have abdicated the crucial role, in both psychology and civilization, of knowing what's best. While our strategic planning in education should always be heavily informed by what the customer wants, we must never as schools abandon our parental role that, sometimes painfully, takes the child from the state of nature into civilized life.

Second, while I have great respect for the conventional strategic-planning process in many situations, its downside is its very logic. That is to say, strategic planning as an exercise tends to lead toward long-term *conclusions*, and that in my judgment is its weakness. There is a tendency after the exercise to end up with a book that tries to nail down a school's destiny three or five or ten years hence. Demographically, economically, curricularly, physically, technologically, where will we be or are we likely to be? Now all of this is useful, but, to the degree that it narrows vision and codifies present facts into future choices, it can also waste a great deal of time, energy, and intellect on documents that five years later are essentially forgotten and unread. Or at worst it can lead to future choices that, when the time comes, should not be made.[2]

Third, and growing directly from my second perspective, valuable as strategic planning in the formal sense can be, I believe that the more important activity is to develop the *habit of strategic thinking*. Management team, administrative cabinet, leadership council, whatever we wish to call it, this group of people has the obligation to engage regularly in strategic thinking. Thus when governance and management issues present themselves, school leaders will have already developed the analytic skills that the wisest solutions to their problems demand.

While the heads of our schools were once expected to do virtually all the strategic thinking, such as it was, the challenge for today's head is to orchestrate strategic thinking, to lead the team in this method of thought, and to supply the discipline that makes sure it happens. Hypothesizing about national and regional trends, about new ideas in education, about local politics and their impact on their school should be a normal part of administrative group meetings. Nearly every week there is an article in national and regional publications, *The Wall Street Journal*, or *The New York Times* that addresses a subject apt for a strategic discussion: single-sex sectioning within a coed school, for-profit corporations entering school management, changes in the tax laws, educational choice including vouchers and tax credits, management trends in corporate America, to name a few. Local possibilities could include property acquisitions, satellite campuses, all manner of curricular and athletic issues, and on and on.

The path to the healthy survival of our schools will be lit by a few good ideas that have survived the strategic critique of talented management teams and, ultimately, of the board of trustees. To me, the exercise of strategic thinking about education and about our schools in particular is the most exciting part of our work. It leads invariably (in Erich Fromm's words) to anticipatory change instead of catastrophic change. It takes energy and commitment, and its quality will ultimately determine the fate of independent education in America.

1. Excerpts from remarks to Team Management Conference, December 1993.

2. It is the same concern that has always led me to recommend against faculty handbooks and other detailed policy manuals in our schools. I don't mind a few guidelines here and there, and the legal obligations that we absolutely have to do, but in the spheres where we have discretion I say don't commit policies, expectations, and acceptable behaviors to print. Because once we have created it, the book takes on a life of its own, rigidifies and becomes dogma, is hard to amend, becomes quickly outdated, and forces us to respect the letter of the law, not its spirit.

CASH FOR SCORES

Bulletin 272, October 2002

The transfer of corporate practices in the for-profit world to independent schools should be handled with extreme care. Some practices such as developing future leaders from within have merit. But one in particular that has become fashionable in the public sector is the concept of bonuses to reward certain kinds of performance. What brings this subject to the fore is the recent announcement by New York City Schools Chancellor Joel I. Klein that superintendents could receive bonuses up to $40,000, "if test scores in their districts significantly improve this year."[1] Turning up the pain, Mr. Klein added that raising test scores should be the paramount goal of city educators. Bonuses, of course, are a form of a prize. Simply put, to award bonuses of any kind in an educational institution is a terrible idea.

Over the years NYSAIS has been asked whether heads or development officers should get bonuses for meeting fund-raising goals. Or whether admissions officers should be rewarded for exceeding enrollment projections. The answer has always been unequivocally no. First, the awarding of cash prizes for one set of accomplishments depreciates all others. Second, bonuses for specific ends may encourage behaviors contrary to accepted good practice, such as bashing other schools or misrepresenting facts. Third, the bonus by its nature soils the culture of a school whose central purpose is the growth and development of children, which in the end can never be attained through a system of bribes.

Revenue sharing, on the other hand, is a different matter. Although it may not reflect the best planning, some schools add a one-time stipend to faculty salaries, for example, in the middle of the year. They do so, presumably, because revenues are higher than expected. But in no case should such payments be called bonuses. If they are, the implication is that the faculty did a better job than anticipated, a highly unlikely event in the course of an ordinary year and an insult to boot. If called a bonus, it would also suggest that each teacher's improved performance was exactly equal to all others. It's much better to be honest and explain that the extra funds are being distributed to a group that cannot be paid enough for the important work they do.

But the worst abomination is to offer prize money to administrators who, in this case, can drive up test scores in the schools. The kind of drilling that such a bonus program engenders may succeed in raising scores on a targeted test, but the whole ugly process can hardly be called education. Imagine a school environment in which chief administrators are competing for cash awards by pressuring teachers to train students for standardized tests. Were it not so close to reality, we would dismiss it as a bad dream. For the time being (and it cannot last), the high-stakes testing craze has hijacked elementary and secondary education in America. Its essential irrelevance to what it means to be an educated man or woman becomes more and more apparent every year. Now that cash for scores has come to New York City and elsewhere, it may be that the testers are getting desperate. In the long run that could be a blessing for our country.

1. Abby Goodnough, "If Test Scores of Students Swell, So May Superintendents' Wallets," *The New York Times*, September 25, 2002.

TO BE AN ADULT

Bulletin 193, November 1994

There are few enough moments of absolute clarity in life, but every once in a while someone says something that reduces a huge reality to a simple line. Psychologist Michael Thompson did it recently, as he spoke to a group of school heads at Mohonk Mountain House. "Only the head," he said, "has to be an adult all the time."

School heads, natively, are surrounded by children. As they should, children act like children. That's the point of being a child. The rest of the school community, faculty, parents, and trustees, are nominal adults. But in a time of job insecurity, guilt-ridden parenthood, and shaky governance, childlike behavior is all too common. The head, resolutely adult to the end, walks the thin line between civilization and anarchy, order and chaos. Rage, tantrums, screaming, even crying are forbidden the head. Only in her car or in his closet or on an analyst's couch may a head indulge.

School heads, the circuit breakers of the institution through which all the current flows, have to keep from snapping all the time. As the wag said, "Someone has to do it." So when anybody asks why the head is paid more, sometimes much more than anyone else, Michael Thompson's elegantly synoptic line is as fine a response as any.

THE MORALITY
OF COMPENSATION

Bulletin 202, October 1995

Recent newspaper stories about a highly compensated college president, namely, Peter Diamondopoulos of Adelphi University, who earns $523,636, have induced apoplexy in certain circles. Since Harvard's president earns $278,000, the critics say, is there not a serious discrepancy? Is there a difference, they ask, between for-profit and nonprofit corporations, and, if so, does it affect management's compensation?

Heads of virtually all organizations are paid more, often substantially more, than anyone else for three major reasons. First, they are held accountable for the entire institution in all its aspects. There is no way out of total responsibility. Second, they must make decisions constantly and relentlessly, something, in truth, that most people abhor doing. Third, the job of chief executive officer is by definition high risk. No quarter given; no mercy asked. Some societies may reward chiefs in other ways. Our society pays.

But in the United States nonprofit corporations are distinguished by several conditions that make them unique. Most nonprofits, including educational institutions, enjoy income, sales, and property-tax exemption. In that sense, they are subsidized by the rest of the citizenry who pay the taxes they don't pay. By law nonprofits may not distribute their "profits" or surpluses to their "stockholders" or stakeholders. All funds that exceed expenses must be reinvested in the enterprise or set aside as reserves. Finally, in the nonprofit world there is an assumption of public service. Tax-exempt status in effect requires that all funds beyond necessary expenses be used to enhance the service.

The question then becomes what are necessary expenses (which obviously include compensation)? If nonprofits are to prosper and perform, they need leaders with talent and endurance who must be paid well. But the nonprofit and for-profit sectors are different. It's morally acceptable to work solely for the money in a for-profit corporation. It's not acceptable in a nonprofit, partly because it's subsidized and partly because there's a duty of public service. So when does the compensation of a chief executive officer in a nonprofit institution become excessive? There is no easy answer, but to paraphrase Justice Potter Stewart who wrote about pornography in a famous case before the Supreme Court, "We can't always define it precisely, but we darn well know it when we see it."

THE PERILS OF RESPONSIBILITY

Bulletin 197, April 1995

I remember vividly the year-end faculty meetings when I was a young teacher. Parts of those gatherings resembled the Committees on Public Safety of the French Revolution. As the various academic and social miscreants were reviewed, we would, out of frustration and exhaustion, vote to send them to the guillotine, which to us meant expulsion. And I remember equally the expression on the headmaster's face as he watched the faculty cull the herd. We were never quite sure whether we were making decisions or recommendations, and when a condemned person showed up in September, our righteous indignation knew no bounds.

At the time, I did not fully understand what was going on. Our view was that the head was soft on difficult students, because he didn't have to deal with them all day. Though he never quite said it, we also resented his implication that if a school has to expel more than an occasional student, the faculty isn't doing its job. We were willing neither to be merciful nor to acknowledge our own failure. But what at least the young among us did not see was that the faculty in its arrogance was trying to exercise power without responsibility. At the end of the meeting we left for summer vacation. It was the head who had to call the families, deliver the news, meet with angry or desperate parents, and explain not how the students had failed but how the school had failed. And though lawsuits were rarer in those days, it was the head who had to protect the school from threats of retribution.

Everyone, of course, would love to have power without responsibility. It's the ultimate fantasy. The paradox of infancy is that to the adult the infant seems powerless and certainly not responsible. But the infant almost achieves the fantasy; she gets fed, clothed, cleaned, cuddled, and warmed on demand. Her sole responsibility is to breathe. Obviously, in the long run we can't have power without responsibility, which may be why so many people are willing to do without either. But in the academic world, which prizes democracy and equality, its leaders are subject to a new malady that threatens our institutions' integrity and survival. It's the worst of all possible conditions: responsibility without power.

Experienced independent-school people regularly lament the shrinking tenure of heads. One able new head, now in her third year, told me she was already planning her departure a year or two hence. Others in the present generation simply assume that the job's vulnerability is so great that no one can last more than a few years. Is it possible that heading a freestanding educational institution in the 1990s has become so complex and enervating that no normally healthy and talented person can stand it for more than a short time? Probably not. What is more likely is that increasing numbers of schools (and colleges, for that matter) have steadily and inexorably diminished the authority of the headship, while leaving it with full responsibility for the fate of the institution. And it does not take long for even the naïve to see that such a circumstance is not only insupportable but unworkable.

In their thirst for collaboration, openness, and equity, many of our schools have stripped decision-making power from those responsible for their welfare. While the trappings and titles remain, the legitimacy of the head's authority has been diluted. Second guessing, endless consultation, and wishy-washy compromise are the order of the day. The diffusion of power either postpones or weakens the hard decisions that move an organization forward. The person left with the responsibility must live with and defend the inadequacy of the outcome. It's an exhausting, soul-destroying role. The difference between the head of my first school and so many of his successors today is that he had the authority to override the "extreme" penalties we imposed. And he often did.

AVERAGES
AND TRANSITIONS

Bulletin 282, October 2003

Headships last from months to decades. No one has yet analyzed in one place all of the ingredients that make or break a headship. It could be a fascinating and possibly useful study, but chances are it would miss some crucial combinations that spell success or failure. In any event, the least important statistic on headships may be their average length: six or seven years. The fallacy of averages is that they suggest to many that the vast majority of heads' tenures is right around the average, say, six and a half years. But like aging (the sixty-five-year-old has a better *statistical* chance of reaching eighty than the fifty-year-old), if a headship reaches six and a half years, it has a better *statistical* chance of reaching ten years than it had at, say, four years. So the likelihood, not yet proven, is that there are a lot more relatively short and relatively long headships than there are average ones, which may be another way of saying that there are more weak and strong headships than there are average ones.

Statistical speculations aside, a critical moment in the life of a school is the transition from old head to new. Generally speaking, the longest tenures create the most difficult transitions. It is a kind of paradox that while very long headships can be good for schools, considerable turmoil often follows, sometimes constructive, sometimes not. The issue lies in the peculiar nature of independent schools: small intentional communities, directly accountable to their constituencies, vulnerable (unlike government schools) to the marketplace. They are solely responsible for their own health and survival. Largely as a result of these circumstances, governing boards of independent schools tend to delegate most of the institution's management to the head. Thus came the old metaphor of the head as the neck in the hourglass. Wherein much is given, much is expected; strong long-term heads become the focal point of a school's healthy survival. And that is the condition that presages the events that follow their departure from the scene.

Long-term heads may or may not be beloved. They can be either the angel or the devil you know. The point is that they represent stability, a predictable pattern, reassurance that the next month or year will be like the last, and, above all, for the low-status profession of teaching in America, job security. It may safely be said that the longer the tenure of heads, the fewer dismissals of faculty and staff. Of course, that could be the consequence of the extraordinary quality of appointments the head has made. But the central fact is that at the end of a lengthy headship, nearly everyone is protecting his territory; the governing board is a smoothly running machine that in varying degrees has lost touch; and the school for the most part is flourishing, on the surface at least. Into this minefield steps the new head, full of hope, passion, even skill, yet almost always without a detector. If only it were as simple as "The king is dead; long live the king." But delegated authority, as we know, is a far different breed than divine. And thus is established the powerful case for the interim headship by design, not default.

THE CASE FOR
INTERIM HEAD

Bulletin 283, November 2003

Unlike decades ago, when the title itself conferred much of a school
head's authority, today's head has to earn most of it. As American
society has in many respects become more democratic, so have
independent schools. Add to that reality the fact that the complexity of heading a school has grown enormously as schools have become
human-service agencies as much as educational institutions, and,
in many cases, the moral center for their constituencies. Thus,
particularly following a lengthy headship in which authority has
been established after years of trust building, cultivation, and collaboration, it becomes problematic at best for a "permanent"
replacement to succeed. The case for the interim headship grows
substantially from the psychological construction and managerial
model of independent schools. Its adoption by governing boards
in the most appropriate circumstances can avoid considerable turmoil, dislocation, and personal pain that in hindsight is unsurprising
but that no one wanted to predict.

Understandably, when boards of trustees face a search for a new
head, they want to get on with it, find the redeemer, and return
to normality. But if ever patience and long-term thinking were
called for, this is the time. Most interim heads are appointed through
default, not design. There simply isn't time to find a permanent
successor for one reason or another. Or the search committee is

dissatisfied enough with the candidates that another year is required to complete the process. But to decide in advance on an interim headship for a year or even two is an act of anticipation that prepares the school for its next cycle of leadership. The belief that a school somehow loses momentum or stature by appointing an interim head, even if true, pales before the myriad benefits of such an appointment.

By far the best interim heads are successful, former heads. Their learning curve is negligible, their judgment is well honed, and they know what is important and what is unimportant in the life of a school. The interim's effectiveness is precisely the result of her disinterest in permanent employment. She serves in the best sense as a consultant to the board of trustees, analyzing the school's strengths and weaknesses, identifying difficult personnel issues, and helping the board with its strategic thinking about next steps. Within the school, the interim manages the administrative team, serves as court of last resort, and generally carries on the day-to-day functions of the head. But above all, his presence, symbolically and otherwise, conveys the message that the old regime is gone, while his tenure gives all the stakeholders time to prepare *emotionally* for the inevitable changes ahead. The role of interim head following a long and stable regime fits the nature of independent schools (small intentional communities, people sensitive, organizationally conservative, self-conscious) to a remarkable degree. It is a role that is as much psychological as it is practical, and in the long run it promotes the healthiest possible transition to the promise of a school's next chapter.

RESPECTING TRUSTEES

Bulletin 198, May 1995

Being a trustee of anything these days takes stamina, where once it didn't take much. The stakes are higher. Exposure is greater. Time is shorter, and demands are bigger. The least we can do for these unpaid volunteers is to husband their time and energy, keep them from boredom, and make their work important. Having a trustee feel superfluous comes close to a cardinal sin. Respecting trustees begins with their meetings. Herewith, a few time-tested suggestions:

1. Be sure that at least one important decision is made at each trustee meeting. Approving routine reports does not qualify. Trustees feel well used if something significant happens, ill used if they merely sit passively like students of old.

2. Try to include at least one important discussion of policy at each meeting. Trustees feel engaged when they participate in policy development to meet changing conditions. They feel disrespected if someone else does their thinking for them.

3. At least two or three times a year schedule a faculty or student report about something educationally significant, such as a departmental curriculum, college placement, a drug program, the teaching of reading, or the uses of technology. A fifteen- or twenty-minute report should be followed by challenging

questions, not just polite chitchat. Those reporting should talk about problems as well as successes. Trustees want the whole truth.

4. Consider reducing the number of full trustee meetings to four per year, each to be an important event with attendance expected. Concurrently, committee meetings may increase slightly and should be highly substantive. If tribal custom requires monthly trustee meetings, never hesitate to cancel those that lack important business. It is insulting to be asked to sit through purely ritual gatherings.

5. Manage time carefully with an eye toward Quaker midnight (10:00 P.M.). Extended, repetitive discussion indulges the few and bores the many. Let the dissidents have a reasonable chance to speak. Thus the minority will feel heard, and the majority will feel that respect has been accorded.

6. Do not allow unanticipated, new subjects to be introduced by trustees with private agendas. Such intrusions are unfair to those who cannot supply responsive information on the spot. They also undermine the meeting's integrity by extending it unacceptably or by limiting discussion of issues that trustees have come prepared to address.

7. Try to arrive at decisions by consensus (which does not necessarily mean unanimity). It is rare that everyone will feel completely comfortable with a decision, but it is equally rare that anyone will try to stand in the way of a carefully prepared initiative. Occasionally, a vote may be necessary, but if so there is no way to avoid the appearance of winners and losers.

8. Once a year ask trustees to evaluate briefly in writing their own meetings. A short form with two or three questions will do. Who knows? Some excellent ideas might spring forth.

HEAD TO HEAD

Bulletin 245, February 2000

In the postmodern independent school there simply is no more important relationship than that of the head and board head. (Which is not to say that a good relationship assures either the skill or effectiveness of either party. That is another issue.) One may ask, has not this always been so? And the answer is yes, but less acutely. The urgencies, the ambushes, and the fragilities of today's school require exquisite communication between head and board head (chair), whereas adequate communication was once enough. The room for slippage has become minuscule.

Just as board chairs may veto the appointment of heads, heads must have the same option for board chairs. No matter how good the intention, there is nothing to be done about terrible chemistry. A fatal flaw in the system is that some heads think their interpersonal skills are impeccable, that they can handle anybody. Not so. It is far more likely that the head will face a succession of board chairs than the other way around. Thus his judgment at every rotation is crucial. If a board imposes a chair, either subtly or bluntly, on a head, it's time to leave.

Assuming a promising start to the head/board chair partnership, the following may be helpful.

Mutual Obligations of Head and Board Chair

- Be sure to discuss and arrive together at exactly what are the head's and board chair's respective responsibilities and prerogatives, keeping in mind that "the head leads the school and the chair leads the board."

- Stay in regular, at least weekly, touch with each other by phone or in person, whether or not there is an immediate problem.

- Keep each other continually aware of policy issues raised by board members, faculty, or community that may require board action.

- Transmit to each other without delay all significant concerns raised by board members or others in the school community.

- Always tell each other as soon as possible about any excellent work she has done or move he has made. There is no such thing as too much deserved praise.

- Always inform each other immediately about serious mistakes in judgment or insensitive or naïve political decisions.

- Be sure that the chair, not the head, has the responsibility for educating board members on trustee etiquette within the community, for example, how to handle complaints, and, when necessary, for disciplining board members who have crossed the line into unacceptable behavior.

- The chair and head should be ex officio members of all board committees and work constantly together on committee structure, assignments, and oversight of agendas.

- The chair and other trustees must take the major responsibility for capital solicitations, though the head must take primary responsibility for cultivating major prospects and must often participate in the final ask.

- The chair is primarily responsible, with other trustees as appropriate, for providing the head with compensation, housing, transportation, and all other benefits commensurate with the importance of his job and the quality of his work.

- The chair, in consultation with the Head, is primarily responsible, with other trustees as appropriate, for designing a system of evaluation for the head's work.

- The chair must assure that the head is fully involved in the nomination of all members and officers of the board of trustees.

- The head must prepare the chair for every eventuality, acquainting him with the earliest signs of trouble and vice versa. Neither party should ever be rudely surprised.

- The head has primary responsibility for telling the school's story and for guarding and promoting the school's mission.

- The head has the responsibility to educate the chair (and board) about every aspect of the school, recognizing the difference between education and domination or manipulation.

- Both parties must remember that they are where they are to serve the students entrusted to their care. The habit of raising the level of discourse always dispels personal agendas.

Obviously, the stakes are high in the matter of head/board chair relations. When the partnership deteriorates and trust evaporates, either the head or board chair leaves, more often the head. But even more important than the personal sacrifice of either one, the school suffers instability and the traumas of reconstruction. In a school of all places, where we model our civilization for the young, there are enough unavoidable obstacles without destroying its leadership by our own inaction.

EVALUATING BOARDS AND HEADS

Bulletin 136, March 1989

In the relatively small world of an independent school nearly everyone knows who is competent, who is adequate, and who is neither. The challenge then is to utilize this knowledge to strengthen the institution on a continuing basis by getting people to perform at or near capacity, and to make personnel changes that will lead to more competency and less adequacy. All of these efforts, to be successful, must be undertaken with a clear understanding of the political limits that the history, character, and self-concept of any one school allow. No small educational community can be run purely as a problem in systems management, but neither can it be managed like a family. Families are wonderful for their purpose, but they are not professional.

If the key leaders in a school (in this case, chairman, board, and head) are competent and confident, informal evaluation of performance is by far the most effective and efficient way to proceed. Formal evaluation, including, as it does, questionnaires, interviews, committee meetings, checklists, etc., reveals in the end all the questions competent people have already asked and all the answers they have already anticipated. It is also a tremendous consumer of time, energy, and intellect that could better be used to improve the fortunes of the school. Finally, for both doctor and patient, it can be boring, boring, boring.

In certain situations, however, formal evaluation can be useful. For a young school or one that is rebuilding after a long decline, formal evaluations can supply a way of rediscovering the basic elements of strength in an institution, of what is important and what is not. All of the paraphernalia of a formal structure in this case compels the participants to think through their educational values and management goals, a vital prerequisite to right decisions. In other words, if a school is floundering for one reason or another, the discipline and focus of formal evaluation may provide the insights necessary to get the school back on course.

Formal evaluation may also be useful if board members, chair, and/or head are inexperienced. Informal evaluation does not work as well when somebody is feeling uncertain, a common problem when one is new. Somehow the formal structure in this instance provides certain handholds that permit the uninitiated to move carefully through the process. On the other hand, the formal approach is occasionally misused when it is deliberately applied to achieve some political end, such as firing the head or purging the board. This means, of course, that the whole concept of evaluation is degraded, since the goal of the exercise is not self-improvement but the removal of certain persons from the organization.

The point is that the method of evaluation of school leaders should reflect the then-current status and conditions of the school. There is no reliable norm good for all seasons and occasions. And as with most other habits of operation, this one should bear constant review.

EVALUATING THE CEO

Bulletin 217, April 1997

Heads of independent schools are presumably the chief executive officers. If they are not, they should be. That's what it means to be responsible for the entire institution. Although the head is evaluated informally every day in countless ways (Does he look tired? Is she morose? Did he sound foolish?), it is the board of trustees' duty to judge the quality of her work. Years of collective experience in this matter have established several sound principles and practices.

First, the head should be evaluated by his employers, not his employees. He is not an elected official. Though generally accountable to the whole community, the head is specifically accountable only to the owners of the school, the trustees who appoint her. Every employee of the school has a narrower focus (mostly much narrower) than the head. Everyone but the head is to some degree a specialist. The head is paid to think about all aspects of the school. It is therefore both unfair and inappropriate to ask employees to evaluate the person whose every decision affects the interests of the whole institution. (If the head wishes to poll faculty and staff on her performance, that is her privilege. It may or may not be helpful.)

Second, the head and board should together each spring determine a set of personal goals for the head and institutional goals for the school to be implemented the following year. The goals should obviously be achievable and reasonable in number since the head is also expected to run the school effectively on a day-to-day basis. It is understood, of course, that the completion of certain goals may require more than a year. Each June a small committee of trustees should meet with the head for an informal discussion of the head's needs, style, stress level, health, and so on and for an evaluation of the head's success in meeting the board-approved goals for the just completed academic year. At the same meeting, goals for the succeeding year should be finalized and put in place.

Third, the head's evaluation should not be coterminous with contract discussions about compensation and benefits. And under no circumstances should goals be included in the language of a head's contract. If the head becomes "legally obligated" to fulfill certain goals, his time and energy are by definition compromised. The notion of incentive pay for heads is also strongly discouraged since such specific links between pay and performance obviate the whole idea of nonprofit governance and the fiduciary roles of head and board.

Last, after a period of years, virtually everybody in a school community knows whether the head is doing a good or good enough job. Both his strengths and, it is hoped, fewer weaknesses are obvious to all, and it is the board's responsibility to make a recurring global judgment about the head's usefulness to the school. In that sense, annual evaluations of a veteran head become somewhat redundant and, if they are conducted at all, become affirmations of what everybody already knows. The danger, after many years of a successful headship, is not that the board foregoes a formal evaluation, but that trustees forget to support the head in personal and professional ways that could make the difference between adequate and excellent performance.

CONTRACTS
PURE AND SIMPLE

Bulletin 148, May 1990

The simplest contract between a head and governing board provides for an extension of compensation beyond the head's departure
in the event of dismissal. It provides basic protection for the head
and her family during the transition to a new job. The simplest
contract may well be enough.

The trouble with all contracts, especially elaborate ones, is that
they assume adversaries and eliminate flexibility, concepts that are
antithetical to everything independent education is supposed to be.
Although a head may feel some modicum of security signing a contract that allows twelve days of sick leave, would he really be content
if the school docked his pay for a thirteenth or fourteenth day in
a given year? Does a head really want to sign a contract that stip-
ulates that if he dies on April 29 his estate will receive one more
day's pay, until the end of the month, before all compensation
ceases? Does she want to sign a paper that spells out the exact number of vacation weeks with no provision for accumulation?

All of these terms and conditions and more are beginning to
show up in heads' contracts, and we know the reasons all too well.
Boards are afraid of choosing the wrong leader for their school
and ending up in a moral and legal quagmire. Heads are afraid that
nervous boards and fickle school communities will leave them
twisting in the wind. But, in the end, if the marriage fails, will all

of the contract's pages have helped resolve the basic issues on which the failure rests? Obviously, massive contracts do not doom the headship, but in not so subtle ways they are monuments to distrust. Unless a school and head will have it no other way, simplest is probably best.

THE FUND-RAISING IMPERATIVE

Bulletin 236, March 1999

One of the happiest traditions in the United States is that it's OK, even respectable, for people who don't have it to ask people who do have it for money. By far the largest percentage of monetary gifts passes from people or foundations to nonprofit corporations, which, if they were not invented in America, have certainly been perfected here. In many respects the nonprofit or charitable corporation is the crucial underpinning of the capitalist system, since it limits government by performing the services that government would otherwise have to provide. It is as though a bargain had been struck that the welfare state may be kept at bay if the for-profit world will fund the nonprofit. In modern America the relationship has become a multibillion dollar undertaking. And long may it survive.

One form, of course, of the nonprofit corporation is the private school. It differs from some others in that the vast majority charge tuition for their services. While it's possible to run a school on tuition alone, the arrangement is self-limiting. You simply cannot charge enough tuition to get the physical quality, the top flight teaching, and the heterogeneous community that most people want. The tuition explosion and its consequence of fewer consumers have already driven several small colleges to cut charges dramatically in the hope of higher enrollments. But, inevitably, if you cut enough, program has to give way somewhere. Thus far most schools have been able to hold the line or at worst make small reductions.

It's hard to know how much charitable giving would suffer if gifts were not tax-deductible. There might still be a great deal. But part of the bargain and the attraction is American tax law, which allows most gifts to pass tax free. Obviously, the higher the tax bracket, the bigger the savings. So it can be argued that the stability of America's social system depends in part on massive charitable giving by accomplishing the transfer of wealth, the provision of public services, and a tendency toward less invasive government. Though not without flaws, it's remarkable how well it all works.

Independent schools, of course, are not exactly social agencies, or are they? But they surely perform a public service. The more money they raise, the greater the service, not only from structural improvements but because a much larger socioeconomic segment of society can attend. Schools are particularly fortunate. They may accept fees tax free to them, and they may accept gifts tax free to the donor. But as both costs and consumer expectations rise, tuition is clearly not enough. No independent school can any longer ignore the fund-raising imperative and the careful recruitment and cultivation of those who by law and tradition bear the major responsibility for attracting donations, namely, our trustees. That we are blessed with so many who care so deeply about our schools and are willing to do this work is indeed a continuing revelation. We must never forget them.

EDUCATION AND MONEY

Bulletin 295, February 2005

The vast disparity in per pupil expense from $3,000 in certain parochial schools to $50,000 or more in some boarding schools begs the question: what is the relationship of money to learning and personal growth, some version of which education is supposed to accomplish? If Utah spends slightly over $5,000 per student and New York over $10,000, as reported by *Education Week*, may we assume that Utah's boys and girls are learning and growing half as much? Not likely. The same, even greater, differences in cost per student exist in private education. Among NYSAIS members alone, tuition in some secondary schools is four times higher than in others. Is the student experience different in the more expensive programs? Without question. Is it four times better in most important respects? Not likely. Could it be worse for a particular child? Possibly.

So what's going on? First, let us admit that no one has yet successfully proven what is essential to the creation of an educated person. It may even be difficult to get agreement on what an educated person is, but it's probably easier than agreeing on how he or she got there. It is, of course, these very uncertainties that make educators vulnerable to pressure from dissatisfied consumers, who push for changes from high-stakes testing to charter schools. Or, back to the price issue, they insist on simply throwing more money at the problem in grand American style and wait to see what happens. The New York City education budget, for example, grew from $8.8 billion to $12.5 billion, or 42%, from 1997 to 2002 with virtually no improvement in academic performance. And, to top it off, the Campaign for Fiscal Equity has gotten the courts to order an additional $5.6 billion for New York City schools. According to *Barron's* magazine, "The city's education budget will reach at least $20 billion within four years for an average per pupil expenditure of more than $18,000 annually." For lots of reasons, it's a frightening scenario.

Returning to our part of the world of organized learning, can we explain the huge disparities in dollars spent per pupil among independent schools? Since we know that there is no clear correlation between extra dollars expended and dramatic improvement in the learning experience, then what is it all about? The unexciting truth appears to be that the higher or lower cost of an independent education is determined by the comfort level of the school's constituency. Today's student, for example, in an elite New England boarding school is surrounded by munificent facilities, grander than many colleges, precisely because the socioeconomic vision of the dominant constituents demands them. Other groups of parents can only afford the basics, solid teaching, academic rigor, and discipline, and they are willing to accept large classes and modest facilities to get them. The inevitable conclusion of this thinking is that the differing costs of elementary and secondary education have little to do with quantifiable performance or, in state educationese, "outcomes," and much more to do with raw market forces.

The reason independent schools work so well therefore has less to do with money spent per student than with their fundamental character. Freestanding institutions, mission driven, directly accountable, and committed to the personal care of each student: these are the indispensable elements of what it means to be an independent school. Each community finally will decide for itself what it wishes to spend to realize its vision of private schooling, once again demonstrating the exercise of free choice. Long may it live.

THE TUITION FRACAS

Bulletin 308, May 2006

Once more this year the press is beating the tuition drums. When increases were announced in late winter for academic year 2006–07, reporters called NYSAIS for commentary as though something astonishing had happened. On March 29 *The Wall Street Journal* ran a front-page story about "sharply" rising tuitions at private schools. The article published median tuitions that compare rates in 2000–01 to those in 2005–06. Nationally, the increase amounts to 14.5% and in New York City 16.5% over a five-year period. If these figures are correct, they would seem modest at worst and barely greater than inflation. So what exactly is all the fuss about?

A few background facts are helpful. Tuitions among NYSAIS' 174 member schools range from free to something in the neighborhood of $30,000.[1] At least two schools charge no tuition, essentially awarding scholarships to all students. Virtually all operating monies are supplied through annual fund-raising or endowment. A few others charge tuition, but have very substantial aid programs so that the average tuition equivalent is low. A number of NYSAIS schools have rates in the $4,000–7,000 range with extremely modest financial aid programs. And many schools are in the $10,000–30,000 group. Tuitions in the elementary grades tend to be lower than high school, particularly in freestanding elementary schools outside of New York City. The point is that given the number of variables among an array of programs, including some twenty boarding schools, it is totally irresponsible to generalize about tuitions.

The problem, we know, is that the media want to shock the public about this issue as though it were immoral to pay a lot of money for a child's education. But there are three things to be said about tuition. First, market and mission drive tuition levels in every respect. Independent schools design their mission according to inner conviction about their population's educational needs and how to construe them. If the school is right in its determination, then the market pays what the mission costs. And within that dynamic and delimited formula, of course, is the secret of independent schools' success. Second, the differences between high- and low-tuition schools are obvious. High-tuition schools will likely have smaller classes, lighter teacher loads, more electives, and more elaborate facilities than low-tuition schools. But is the $30,000 education by all measures six times better than the $5,000 education? Very unlikely. Again the point is that each family is getting essentially what it wants. Third, though it's still a free country and people can talk about anything they want, tuitions are really nobody's business except those who charge them and those who pay them. Tuitions are basically a socioeconomic contract between educational providers and users. For heaven's sake, let's leave them alone to decide on the terms, as we do every other transaction in life. Please, no more whining.

1. Special-focus schools often exceed $30,000.

PAYING IN
AND PAYING OUT

Bulletin 113, November 1986

As heads, business officers, and boards undertake the annual rite of budgeting (for 1987–88), they are faced once again with the question that will not go away: how does the school reconcile the imperative for higher salaries with the need for reasonable tuitions? Policy-makers may wish to include some of the following points in their thinking.

1. Schools with a normal teacher load of eighty students can pay more than schools with a normal load of fifty or sixty. There is no conclusive study showing that students in a class of fifteen learn more than students in a class of twenty solely on the basis of numbers.

2. Independent-school teacher salaries lost ground in the 1970s and early 1980s both absolutely and relatively. Given the native ability and richness of education required for competence as a teacher, salaries remain egregiously low compared to other professions.

3. Schools with tuitions that are lower than the prevailing market are often perceived not as bargains, but as institutions that must have something wrong with them. To be cheap in America is no longer to be virtuous.

4. Is there a sizable portion of the school's constituency that could easily pay substantially more that the present rates? If so, the

children of that underpaying group are being subsidized by the "free" labor of the faculty and staff. High tuition with generous financial aid is ultimately the fairest system for all concerned, since each family pays according to its ability.

5. Quality should govern price. Tuition rates did not come down from Olympus. They have evolved haphazardly and are generally arbitrary. The question is, "What is a superior service worth, and are we charging appropriately?" BMW automobiles do not sell for $7,500.

6. If all else fails, calculate your tuition on a daily basis. A $7,000 tuition for 180 days comes to $38.88 per day; a $4,000 tuition for 170 days amounts to a mere $23.52 per diem. Expensive? Why it's practically a giveaway.

WHITHER TUITIONS AND SALARIES?

Bulletin 134, December 1988

The annual debate about tuitions and salaries is well under way. How do schools keep the former reasonable and the latter respectable? Is there a theoretical point beyond which parents will not pay and below which teachers will not work? To make parents and teachers happy, the options for schools are limited and difficult. Increasing student-teacher ratios produces more tuition dollars for salaries, but many schools feel bound by history and philosophy not to take that step. Increasing teacher loads accomplishes the same end, but many schools do not relish the hostility that such a move unleashes. Building endowment for faculty salaries, while the least controversial approach, is also the least likely, since most schools cannot raise enough to make a substantial difference.

And so we return to some unpleasant truths. Independent-school tuitions are approaching, and in some cases exceeding, private-college tuitions. In the final analysis, schools can only charge what the market will bear. After falling behind in the 1970s, teacher salaries have made progress in the 1980s, though they are hardly generous. Unless American attitudes change profoundly, and nothing profound happens quickly, among the professions teacher salaries will not soon match those of doctors, lawyers, or engineers. To some degree, teaching as a career in the United States will remain a calling.

Thus the perennial questions: what do we do about faculty compensation? First, we recognize that the issue is not fundamentally managerial or economic or political. Fundamentally, it is a moral issue. When heads and trustees finally decide on next year's teacher salaries, let them ask themselves without obfuscation and without rationalization: are we doing the best we can?

THE TUITION DEBATE

Bulletin 268, May 2002

At a recent meeting outside New York State the head of a prominent East Coast school said that his board had raised tuition 7%,
along with a 20% increase in applications. One of this head's
predecessors back in the mid-twentieth century used to say that
he would tell the board each year, "We have to raise tuitions."
And every year someone would say, "But what's going to happen if we raise tuitions?" (This meant, will there be a rebellion?)
Every year the head would say, "Nothing is going to happen!"
and nothing did. The tuition argument continues to dog independent schools, yet none of the essential facts have changed.
Let it be said right up front, dear reader. It's a mistake to try to
keep tuitions low, that is, below the market.

Acknowledging a few exceptions, such as certain religious schools
that are effectively subsidized by their denominations or neighborhood schools that specifically serve low-income families, it is not
possible to have a first-class school with a second- or third-class
revenue stream. The vast majority of schools do not have an endowment large enough to make up for low tuitions, nor can successful
annual giving do the trick, because it has long been a general item
of income in most operating budgets. It's hard enough to run a
good school on the backs of poorly paid teachers and staff. To try
to do it with low tuitions as well is a doomed undertaking that ultimately invites either mediocrity or unjustifiable sacrifice.

Tuition guilt stems from the liberal character of independent-school people. Most independent schools were founded as an entrepreneurial act, based on the idea of a person or group, to be offered as a service in the market. This, of course, is the essence of the capitalist system, which dictates that all goods and services should be sold at what the market will bear. The higher the quality, the higher the price. Schools that charge significantly lower tuition, often with little or no financial aid, argue that a larger slice of the "middle" class can thus afford the cost. Maybe so, but within the total socioeconomic spectrum of America, it's still a very small slice. Three things happen with low tuitions. First, those who could easily pay higher tuitions get an unearned discount. Not paying what you can afford is in this case a fundamentally immoral position. Second, there is little or no money for real socioeconomic diversity, which includes students from *all* classes. Third, teaching, already a low-status profession, suffers even more from painfully inadequate salaries.

The vast majority of private independent schools, and private colleges for that matter, serve the high end of society. In that sense, they are indisputably elitist, which needs no apology. There is somewhere in the great blue sky an absolute minimum number of dollars per student required to run a top school. Private independent schools are better than most government schools in part because they cost more per student. (The for-profit, of all things, Edison Project is discovering this hard truth.) The central question for our schools is not whether we are elitist, but whether we care about other segments of society. The only way to be excellent and to bring all classes into our schools is to charge what the upper echelons of the market can afford. Then everyone is served by quality, by fairness, and by redistribution. NYSAIS schools alone spend $100 million per year on financial aid. Those precious funds are not produced from low tuitions.

SMALL CLASSES, GREAT TEACHING

Bulletin 125, February 1988

Independent-school leaders regularly deplore low teacher salaries. But despite outcries each year, there is a kind of fatalism attached to the issue that seems to defy all attempts at a solution. Higher tuitions simply "maintain" salary levels. Other professions seem able to leap ahead faster, thus widening the gap. Education is personnel intensive and therefore cannot improve "productivity" as business corporations can. Except for the richest schools, with vast endowments and prodigious annual giving, there is simply no way to effect significant change.

Yet everyone knows that for most private schools with high tuitions and mainstream programs, the root cause of low salaries lies in the teacher-student ratio. For years schools have boasted small classes, implying, for example, that more learning goes on in a room with one teacher and twelve students than in a room with one teacher and eighteen students. But aside from the fact that no study has ever shown that claim to be true, would anyone prefer to have his child in a classroom of twelve with a competent teacher than in a classroom of eighteen with a great teacher? In many cases, independent schools have become prisoners of their own marketing and their own myth.

In the long run, families will flock to schools where great teaching is the norm no matter how big the classes. And in the long run, great teaching will be easier both to obtain and demand in schools that pay high salaries. Perhaps the time has come for certain schools to change their marketing strategy from small classes to great teaching and to take the steps that transform image into reality.

MISGUIDED PRIORITIES

Bulletin 142, October 1989

As middle and upper schools feel the pinch of declining birthrates in the 1970s and parents complain more vociferously about rising tuitions, board and heads wonder if the shrinkage of the applicant pool is permanent. Are independent schools systematically doomed to a long decline? Have we at last reached our apogee in the marketplace of American education?

Improving birthrates in the 1980s offer some short-term relief, but what about tuitions? Are there enough families with "discretionary" income to support existing independent schools in New York State? A conservative estimate indicates that about 40,000 families send children to NYSAIS schools. Of those, conservatively again, about 35,000 pay full tuition, a startlingly small number in a state with the eighth-largest economy in the world. (California is seventh.)

The fact is that there are tens of thousand of New York families who could by any reasonable standard afford to send children to NYSAIS schools, but choose not to. Some send their offspring to public schools for ideological or personal reasons, but many simply send them to save money for consumer items that far exceed necessity. Thorstein Veblen's eyes would pop if he could see the material possessions that smother the American middle-class family today.

Our relatively genteel tradition still argues against making certain points, as we, perish the thought, market our schools. Yet as

American corporations begin to spend millions of dollars reeducating thousands of entry-level employees whose mostly public education has left them functionally helpless, there are points to be made. Postpone the BMW for a Hyundai (if it has to be foreign); the difference can pay many tuitions. Cut the club memberships in half. Take domestic vacations. Redo the kitchen some other time. Invest in your children's education now, for heaven's sake, or they may have no choices to make in adulthood. Remember that the time to spend money on education is during the school years. If children have the foundation, college will take care of itself.

It's time for independent schools to hammer home the truth about the wreckage of American schooling today. The work we do with young people, who are no less educable in the 1990s than they ever were, is simply too important to be missed, especially by those who can afford it with just a little deprivation elsewhere. We have an obligation to make parents feel the consequences of educational neglect. Our deteriorating society demands no less.

REFLECTIONS

Bulletin 115, January 1987

Finding great teachers has never been easy and never will be. So far the vaunted teacher shortage has not reached most NYSAIS schools. The supply of strong candidates for nearly all subject areas and levels continues to be plentiful. Stories of young men and women leaving careers in the law and finance to teach are no longer rare, and many schools can claim at least one former head among their classroom practitioners.

Knowing that our salaries and facilities are modest by the standards of the corporate world, that the status of teachers in America has always been low, and that at no time in our history has so much been expected of teachers, how do we explain the availability of so many good people? What is it about the nature of our communities that attracts men and women who could make a better living elsewhere? And how much of our appeal can be related to changes in the world beyond our schools? We could, presumably, learn a lot about independent education from the answers to those questions.

PERFORMANCE PAY

Bulletin 123, November 1987

Most teachers and many heads prefer salary systems that avoid special increments for performance (some say, merit). Trustees tend to feel different. The argument for performance pay is well-known. People who perform better, who "produce" more, should be paid more. The problem is that a teacher's performance, except in gross terms, is hard to measure. What may seem routine in a classroom today may be identified as decisive years later by a grateful former student. To get agreement of the exact efficacy of complicated human interactions is a daunting challenge. Thousands of faculty committees that have tried to invent instruments that measure performance would so testify.

The arguments against performance pay are several. First, teachers comprise a unique culture. They are for the most part highly educated, strongly egalitarian, and notably underpaid. Most believe that performance pay pales before the issue of a decent standard of living for all, that it amounts to cynical diversion from the essential injustice. Second, if initial evaluations of new teachers are rigorous and prolonged, the likelihood of wide variations among the experienced teachers is sharply reduced. Third, rather than pay the "better" teachers more, counsel out the "poorer" teachers and pay everyone who's left a little more. Fourth, reward good teaching in other ways, through recognition, better conditions, or professional opportunities.

Generally speaking, the more distant the observer from the inside of a school, the more likely he is to favor performance pay. This is not to say that the insiders are right in their opposition. In theory, at least, the American system rewards high-quality work with extra money. Should teachers be treated differently? Perhaps not. But a case can be made that under the peculiar circumstances of the teaching profession in America, performance pay does not produce the incentives in schools that it is designed to produce in all other places.

LOSING OUR FACULTIES

Bulletin 247, April 2000

The ancient joke that "old school heads never die; they just lose their faculties," may seem less funny as independent schools actually face the loss of superior teachers. For decades our schools have talked about attracting and holding great teachers in the confident belief that the challenge was skillful selection, not limited supply. The not unjustified conceit at the heart of our confidence was that government schools could never compete with the quality of professional life in ours. And for a long time, despite big differences in pay, that view of the world has been essentially borne out. Sad to say, the worm may be turning.

Math and science teachers (and, more recently, Spanish teachers) have been hard to find for years. But for the first time in memory, many report, the overall pool of top talent from preschool to twelfth grade is shrinking. What has changed? First, salaries in the best public schools are in the high five figures. A first-grade teacher in Westchester County can earn over $80,000. Second, higher education, law, and medicine continue to exact their toll. But third, and most important, the talented young are flocking to jobs in the "new economy" at salaries that take their parents' breath away. Teaching in America is a low-status profession, but there are those, thank heaven, who still want to do it. The question for us is how do we make it possible for the best and the brightest to do what they want to do?

Acknowledging that independent schools will never catch up in raw compensation with the richest public schools, what else is there to attract and hold great teachers? A few suggestions:

1. Build into the salary system a merit pay component. Being against merit pay is a low-status attitude. Talented people like merit pay and deserve it.

2. Enhance the professional-development budget. It is a respectful act to send deserving people to workshops, institutes, and conferences of real quality.

3. Develop a short leave (not sabbatical) program for teachers of proven worth and longevity, for example, three months before or after summer. There should be no strings attached and full pay. The purpose is refreshment of the recipient's choice. The only cost to the school is the cost of a substitute.

4. Offer supplementary retirement benefits that exceed the school's normal program. Teachers deserve more than minimalist conditions in old age.

5. Make interest-free loans available for down payments on a house. Thousands of teachers who work in cities and boarding schools have no equity in real estate.

6. Consider helping faculty with tuition payments for their children at other schools or colleges. Federal law permits such grants tax free.

7. Provide faculty members with an occasional consultant for personal financial and estate planning. Academic people especially need to know how to stretch limited resources. Several schools have successfully undertaken such a program.

All of the above can be financed through relatively modest endowment funds, foundation grants, or a slice of tuition income. Felicitous working conditions and an environment of intimacy are still the main attractions of independent schools for teachers. But we must find ways to add even more value to the chronically low-paying profession of teaching, especially in a country where status is measured by wealth, not vocation. It is indeed a cliché that great teachers are the sine qua non of our schools, yet it is a cliché because it is true.

THE CASE FOR PERFORMANCE

Bulletin 287, April 2004

One of the paradoxes of independent schools is that heads and most major administrators are compensated based on merit, while teaching faculty generally is not. The trend toward mindless step systems or salary scales of one kind or another has sadly accelerated over recent decades. The consequence, of course, is that experienced teacher A, who gives 50% more in time and talent than experienced teacher B, is paid either exactly or close to the same as her colleague. Heads, desperate to circumvent this absurdity, try to find circuitous ways through perks, supplements, and such to keep a good person or attract a rare one. But even this method is often futile and, in any case, fundamentally dishonest. The argument that an egalitarian salary system simply requires careful supervision so that all teachers are equally strong doesn't play for two reasons. First, virtually no independent school could or would conduct a hiring and firing program ruthless enough to accomplish the goal. And second, there aren't alpha teachers enough in the world that more than a few schools could have a crew of the very best under any circumstances. But that's only part of the story.

Teaching, as we know, is a low-status profession in America. Why else would public-school teachers (and some private) have chosen the industrial-union model as their method of representation with management? Industrial unions originated in the nineteenth and early-twentieth centuries as a way for oppressed workers to survive and be heard. Unions make a point of herding their members into a mass to protest low wages or poor working conditions and to conduct strikes, if necessary. Generally speaking, unions promote pay scales that disallow distinctions based on competence and productivity. Seniority, on the other hand, becomes the governing mantra. Thus two things happen. Talent is unrewarded, and mediocrity is protected. Though the vast majority of independent schools are not unionized, the same mentality dominates our compensation systems. Because of low-status attitudes, even our teachers prefer salary arrangements connected primarily to time served, not performance. And most heads, to the consternation of their boards, succumb to Sam Rayburn's famous admonition, "If you want to get along, go along."

Let it be said that no serious person is advocating a pure merit system for faculty salaries. Certainly, there should be a cost-of-living factor, not necessarily pegged to the index, and possibly some step increases in the early years. But at least a third of the annual salary appropriation should be connected to performance. At this point someone asks: "But is it worth rocking the boat?" And the answer is unequivocally, yes! And this is why. First, confident, talented people in any profession like merit pay, though they may be intimidated by insecure colleagues. Second, the absence of performance-based compensation actually perpetuates low-status attitudes both within the schools and in the outside world, because time-served pay is equated with survival, not accomplishment. At its heart it serves insecurity, not self-confidence. Third, a merit system tends to advance the whole pay scale faster, because the school's goal is to pay the highest high salaries, not just the highest median. Talented, unafraid, aspiring teachers who know they will be rewarded for excellence strengthen the whole profession.

What is absolutely essential is that our independent schools especially do not conspire to keep teaching a low-status profession by allowing compensation systems that discourage talent and protect ordinariness. Strangely, as the union mentality has retreated significantly in the rest of society, it has become more entrenched in schools. It's time to start reversing the tide, and with conviction and, yes, education, our schools can do it.

TEACHING TOWARD DESTITUTION

Bulletin 145, February 1990

Teachers, among many others, are not particularly sophisticated about investing money and planning for their financial futures. Nor, need one point out, are they among the most highly paid professional class in America. As medical costs rise and inflation persists, there is nothing sadder than an aging teacher who faces genteel destitution in retirement. Unfortunately, most schools can't do very much to help their oldest faculty at this late date, but there are ways to help the young and middle aged to get the most from limited resources.

There was a time, as many now lament, when managing all of life was simpler. Choices were fewer. Wheaties, Cheerios, and cornflakes were the basic fare. Now there are hundreds from which to choose. The world of personal finance was just as simple. A checking account, savings account, and social security summed it up. Now the financial choices are staggering. Even good old TIAA-CREF, which chugged along for thirty-five years with two funds, is now in the throes of multiple births. Understanding the vast array of "opportunities" is hard enough for the experts, not to speak of people whose primary concerns are elsewhere.

What a few schools have done, and more should do, is provide faculty and staff with organized financial counseling. Sensible financial decisions, even when small amounts are involved, can make a tremendous difference. Many school people need guidance in such areas as drafting a financial plan, saving for higher education, investment decisions, the best kinds of insurance, retirement income, and estate planning. Providing a counseling program for interested faculty and staff need not break the bank. A visiting professional can cover the major topics in large group seminars for a reasonable fee. And for its modest investment the school ends up with faculty and staff that feel more secure about their future and whose heightened morale must redound to the children in their care.[1]

---

1. While NYSAIS does not endorse specific financial counseling firms, it may have suggestions for schools to explore.

WHY TUITION REMISSION

Bulletin 186, March 1994

Teachers and administrators who are parents obviously love tuition remission, which means a tax-free, subsidized education for their children in the school where they work. Schools may also pay tuition at other equivalent institutions for their staff's children if they so wish. They may not, however, pay college tuitions. The law on this subject is clear.

Lately, a number of schools have considered cutting tuition remission as a way of saving money. Some seek to eliminate it; others to curtail it. Few are introducing or expanding it. Critics of tuition remission claim that it is a discriminatory benefit and that it places an extra burden on nonfaculty parents who have to make up the difference. At worst, they say, it subsidizes certain well-to-do teachers who could easily foot the bill. But despite these concerns, the case for tuition remission remains compelling.

From the institutional viewpoint tuition remission has only one purpose: to attract and hold the strongest possible full-time *teachers* and *administrators* who are also parents. While some of our greatest educators are and have been childless, and while schools need the talent and commitment of childless adults, they require also a critical mass of professional staff with the experience of parenthood. Especially in a time of family disintegration, it is important to have strong, committed parents among those who work with our children.

The difference between tuition remission and financial aid is that the former is automatic, no questions asked. Professional staff with children are spared the indignity of baring their financial souls to insider committees and school heads, who will decide if they qualify. More important, their standard of living is left intact, and they are not penalized for having children, without whom there would be no schools. Assuming salary equity for all teachers and administrators, tuition remission may be seen not as a benefit but as a means of maintaining equal spendable income for staff with and without children.

As for subsidizing rich faculty members, not only is the condition comparatively rare, but such people may be asked frankly if they would consider waiving their right. Some may also be moved to contribute generously to capital campaigns or annual giving. If nonfaculty parents complain, they may be asked if they would prefer weaker teachers or a school in which no staff member had school-age children. Finally, tuition remission is one of the last "benefits" left that is unambiguously tax free and easy to administer. Schools should think extremely carefully before abandoning or curtailing it. Those without it may even consider its introduction.

EDUCATING
THE EDUCATED

Bulletin 275, February 2003

Some call it professional development, others continuing education, but, whatever the nomenclature, we know what it means.
Adult professionals are expected to attend a variety of programs
that acquaint them with the latest in their fields. MDs, LLDs, CPAs,
even personal trainers are required periodically to take a minimum
number of courses to retain certifications or licenses. In New
York State, public-school teachers must obtain the master's degree
within five years of beginning teaching with more to follow (though
we know there is no connection per se between the holding of
degrees and competency in the classroom). Only in private schools,
true to their libertarian tendencies, are there no absolute requirements for extended education beyond the bachelor's degree. The
question, of course, is what is the value of all of this except to maintain at all costs the credentials industry.

The truth is that we do not know exactly what the benefits of
professional development are. The learning experts tell us that we
forget 80% of everything we learn within five years. But that is
not surprising. People who teach report that they do not master
their subject until they teach it, for the simple reason that they use
it every day. Just as all great teachers have high EQs (emotional
quotients), it may very well be that the emotional value of professional development is at least as important as the intellectual. First,
allowing or encouraging a teacher or administrator to attend a

workshop or conference is in itself an act of respect, particularly in an underpaid profession. It says that they are worth the inconvenience and cost for an opportunity for refreshment, colleagueship, and, just possibly, a small epiphany. Second, it places value on the profession by suggesting that teaching is not static but dynamic and evolving. Indeed, the same old notes and techniques will not do. And third, though no single idea may transform a career, the corporate act of attending a professional event is a powerful reminder that failing to examine critically what we do each day is a perilous course. As with most other human activities, it is the cumulative effect of continuing education that has major impact.

The National Association of Independent Schools has long recommended that at least 1% of a school's budget should support professional development. While some schools meet or exceed that number, many do not. Clearly, heads of school must be committed to sending faculty and staff into the wider world of competing ideas and emotional awakening, or it will not happen. The risk is small, and the possible benefits substantial. For, after all, if we do not believe in growth and change, then what is the point of the work we do?

CONTRIBUTORS

DREW CASERTANO
President, NYSAIS, 2005–present

Drew Casertano grew up in Cheshire, Connecticut, where he attended public school and the Cheshire Academy. He completed his high-school years at the Choate School in Wallingford. A graduate of Amherst College in Massachusetts, Drew received an EdM from the Harvard Graduate School of Education, Cambridge. He began his career in education at the Loomis Chaffee School in Windsor, Connecticut, where he taught history, ran a dormitory, and coached football, hockey, and lacrosse. He then served as director of admissions at the Gunnery in Washington, Connecticut. In 1990 Drew was appointed the sixth head of the Millbrook School, a coed boarding and day high school in New York. He continues in that role today. Drew and his wife, Linda, herself a seasoned independent-school faculty member, have three sons.

CHARLES F. HERTRICK
President, NYSAIS, 2001–2003

Chuck Hertrick grew up in Pittsburgh. He holds a BA in English from Lafayette College, Easton, Pennsylvania; an MA in English from Carnegie Mellon University, Pittsburgh; and an EdM from the Harvard Graduate School of Education, Cambridge. Chuck began his career in education as an English teacher at Sewickley Academy in Pennsylvania. In 1974 he became the English department chair at Greenwich Country Day School in Connecticut, where he was also director of secondary-school placement. He subsequently joined the faculty of Thayer Academy in Braintree, Massachusetts, where he taught English and was college-placement director and director of admissions. Since 1988 Chuck has been head of the Allendale Columbia School, a pre-K–12 coed day school in Rochester, New York. (He began there as the head of its upper school.) Chuck and his wife, Joan, have been married for thirty-two years. Currently attending Williams College in Williamstown, Massachusetts, their son, Scott, was a "lifer" at Allendale Columbia School.

DOROTHY A. HUTCHESON
President, NYSAIS, 2003–2005

Dorothy Hutcheson grew up in Atlanta and graduated from the Westminster Schools. She holds an AB in English and religion from Duke University, Durham, North Carolina, and an MSEd in counseling from Duquesne University, Pittsburgh. From 1980 to 1987 she taught English and served as associate director of college counseling, assistant head form advisor, and housemaster at Shady Side Academy in Pittsburgh. She spent the next five years at the Packer Collegiate Institute in Brooklyn, New York, where she served as interim head, assistant head for external affairs, college counselor, and dean of students. Since 1992 Dorothy has been head of the Nightingale-Bamford School, a K–12 girls school in New York City. She also teaches public speaking to juniors. Dorothy lives in New York City with her husband, Sam, who is the director of outreach at St. Peter's Lutheran Church, and their daughter, Holly, who is a member of Nightingale-Bamford's class of 2011.

ANDREW MCLAREN
President, NYSAIS 1997–1999

Born in Scotland and raised there and in England, Andrew McLaren earned a BA in history from Trinity College in Cambridge and an MA in educational psychology from Teachers College, Columbia

University in New York City. He taught at St. Bernard's School in New York City from 1962 to 1970, simultaneously serving as head of its lower school for most of that period. Andrew then took a short intermission from schools and worked as an advertising copywriter. From 1973 to 2004 Andrew served as head of school at, successively, the Dutchess Day School in Millbrook, New York; Tuxedo Park School, New York; and Little Red School House and Elizabeth Irwin High School in New York City. He currently serves as associate executive director of the New York State Association of Independent Schools, and frequently gives workshops for independent school boards on governance and strategic planning. Andrew lives in New Canaan, Connecticut, with his wife, Francie Irvine, who is assistant head of New Canaan Country School. He has three children, who are, Andrew says, all glad to be at least temporarily out of the world of education.

LUCY SCHNEIDER
Trustee, NYSAIS, 1997–2004

Lucy Schneider grew up in New York City and is a graduate of the Packer Collegiate Institute in Brooklyn, New York. She holds a BA in philosophy from Vassar College, Poughkeepsie. Lucy taught at the Rudolf Steiner School, a pre-K–12 coed school in New York City, for twenty-two years, serving as faculty chair for fifteen of those years. Recently retired from full-time teaching, she is currently mentoring new teachers and consulting at Waldorf schools around the country. Her two children graduated from the Rudolf Steiner School.

ARCHIBALD A. SMITH III
President, NYSAIS, 1999–2001

Arch Smith grew up in Texas, graduating from St. John's School in Houston. He holds a BS from Trinity College, Hartford, Connecticut, and an MALS from Wesleyan University, Middletown, Connecticut. He is completing his thirty-second year at the Trinity-Pawling

School, a boarding and day school for boys from seventh through twelfth grades in Pawling, New York. Before being appointed head-master in 1990, Arch served as assistant headmaster and director of college placement and also taught chemistry. Arch and his wife, Gay, who partners with him in leading the Trinity-Pawling community, have three grown sons.